W9-BOL-310

THE

CATHOLIC

VISION FOR

LEADING LIKE
JESUS

THE CATHOLIC VISION FOR

LEADING LIKE JESUS

Introducing S³ Leadership
Servant, Steward, Shepherd

OWEN PHELPS, PH.D.
FOREWORD BY KEN BLANCHARD

Our Sunday Visitor Publishing Division
Our Sunday Visitor, Inc.
Huntington, Indiana 46750

Nihil Obstat
Rev. Mark Gurtner, J.C.L.
Censor Deputatus

Imprimatur
✠ John M. D'Arcy
Bishop of Fort Wayne-South Bend
January 30, 2009

The *Nihil Obstat* and *Imprimatur* are official declarations that a book is free from doctrinal or moral error. It is not implied that those who have granted the *Nihil Obstat* and *Imprimatur* agree with the contents, opinions, or statements expressed.

Every reasonable effort has been made to determine copyright holders of excerpted materials and to secure permissions as needed. If any copyrighted materials have been inadvertently used in this work without proper credit being given in one form or another, please notify Our Sunday Visitor in writing so that future printings of this work may be corrected accordingly.

Copyright © 2009 by Owen Phelps. Published 2009.

14 13 12 11 10 09   1 2 3 4 5 6 7 8 9

All rights reserved. With the exception of short excerpts for critical reviews, no part of this work may be reproduced or transmitted in any form or by any means whatsoever without permission in writing from the publisher. Contact: Our Sunday Visitor Publishing Division, Our Sunday Visitor, Inc., 200 Noll Plaza, Huntington, IN 46750; 1-800-348-2440; bookpermissions@osv.com.

ISBN: 978-1-59276-605-5 (Inventory No. T888)
LCCN: 2009921979

Cover design by Lindsey Luken
Interior design by Sherri L. Hoffman

PRINTED IN THE UNITED STATES OF AMERICA

To my helpmate, partner, friend, and lover, Jane, whose selfless gift of her life to me in marriage has made my life and my work more generative and gratifying than I ever dared to dream. Of God's many great gifts to me, you are surely the greatest. Thank you.

When I look at your heavens, the work of your fingers,
    the moon and the stars that you have established;
what are human beings that you are mindful of them,
    mortals that you care for them?

Yet you have made them a little lower than God,
    and crowned them with glory and honor.
You have given them dominion over the works of your hands;
    you have put all things under their feet,
all sheep and oxen,
    and also the beasts of the field,
the birds of the air, and the fish of the sea,
    whatever passes along the paths of the seas.

O LORD, our Sovereign,
    how majestic is your name in all the earth!

PSALM 8:3-9

Table of Contents

Foreword

When Phil Hodges and I first began to discuss the idea of developing tools to help people *lead like Jesus*, we knew we didn't want to develop just another leadership program. Our vision was to launch a *movement*.

We wanted to share our conviction that Jesus is the greatest leadership role model of all time, and that everyone can learn to lead as Jesus did. To accomplish this, we would need to produce some materials to help us spread the word. And yet, we wanted to avoid the implication that there was a neat little package of information that guaranteed anyone could lead like Jesus.

We recognized that leading like Jesus involves, first and foremost, matters of the heart. To lead like Jesus, one needs a servant's heart. I'm not saying that in order to be an effective leader one has to first become entirely selfless. I'm saying that to develop our aptitude to lead like Jesus, we have to recognize our fundamental self-centeredness and commit ourselves daily to becoming ever more God's servant in the image of Jesus' own character.

We recognized, too, that over the centuries Jesus' followers had let themselves become divided over various issues. We committed ourselves to avoiding the pitfalls of divisiveness and remaining faithful to Jesus' own wish "that they may all be one" (Jn 17:21). We resolved that the Lead Like Jesus movement would always be "nondenominational and nondoctrinal." That commitment is at the core of who we are and all we do.

At the same time, we recognized that the faith experience of many people is different. Not only should we respect the Christian experience of other Christians, we should reach out to them and build partnerships to spread the Lead Like Jesus message. To make these partnerships effective, we knew we would have to customize the Lead

Like Jesus message to resonate with the lived Christian experience of different people.

The Catholic Vision for Leading Like Jesus is an effort to do just that. Its purpose is not to revise the principles we present in the Lead Like Jesus movement, but only to enhance them for a particular audience — the more than 1 billion Catholics in the world who proclaim Jesus Christ as their Lord and Savior.

I am pleased that we have found a member of the Lead Like Jesus movement who is a Catholic family man to step up and take on this task. Owen Phelps, a certified Lead Like Jesus facilitator, has worked for his church for a quarter of a century and has excellent credentials in both the fields of religious studies and leadership training.

It is our hope that others will step forward in the days ahead to help us develop more partnerships of all kinds in other faith traditions. In that way, our vision of Lead Like Jesus as a movement will flower and grow. And even more important than that, we will all be better servants of God.

KEN BLANCHARD

About This Book

This book is not the definitive text on how to lead like Jesus. We believe the definitive text is *Lead Like Jesus: Lessons from the Greatest Leadership Role Model of All Time*, by Ken Blanchard and Phil Hodges, co-founders of the Lead Like Jesus movement.[1] We recommend that all Christians read this book and try to incorporate its principles into their everyday relationships at home, at work, and in their communities. Were it not for Ken and Phil's work in that book and in their Lead Like Jesus Encounters, this book could not have been written. This book represents an effort to affirm Ken and Phil's insights about how Jesus calls us to lead and to develop those insights further in light of Catholic teaching, tradition, and experience.

For example, Ken and Phil insist that everyone is called to be a leader. We agree. Because we recognize that Catholicism sees married life as a true vocation and places a great emphasis on the value of families in building a just society and a vital faith community, you will find sections called "In the Family" scattered throughout this book. In these we explore various facets of the call to lead like Jesus in our homes. You will also find sections called "On the Job," "In the Community," and "In the Church" sprinkled throughout, where we explore Christlike leadership in those specific contexts.

You will also find that we expand the concept of *servant leadership* to include *steward leadership* and *shepherd leadership*, uniting the three under the banner of S³ Leadership. Our purpose is not to dilute the core insight, captured so well in Scripture and explained so clearly by Ken and Phil, that *Jesus calls us to be servant leaders*. Rather, our purpose is to add two legs to help balance and stabilize that great truth so that we all might live better, love more, and build the kingdom as Jesus did — with the heart of a true servant leader focused on fulfilling the will of God.

Introduction

Let your adornment be the inner self with the lasting beauty of a gentle and quiet spirit, which is very precious in God's sight.

1 Peter 3:4

For months, I struggled with a choice. Should I develop my concepts of leading like Jesus around the notion of *servant* or *steward*? Then one day I started to wonder: *Are you crazy? Why choose one when both are essential?* The concept of S² Leadership was born.

Some months later, I was in an elevator with Ken Blanchard and Phil Hodges, co-founders of the Lead Like Jesus movement. We were on the University of San Diego campus headed to meet a graduate class being taught by Ken and his wife, Margie. I saw an opportunity to share my story about the agonizing but ultimately false choice between *servant* and *steward*.

"Why not make it S³ Leadership?" Ken asked.

"S³?" I asked. I wasn't sure what he was getting at.

"Servant, steward, and shepherd," he proposed. In that moment the concept of S³ Leadership was born.

A very good way to understand and appreciate Jesus' approach to leadership — His teaching and His example — is to see it in terms of the S³ framework.

- He practiced *servant* leadership.
- He saw his leadership role as a *steward*.
- He cared for His disciples as a *shepherd* cares for his sheep.

If you are committed to these dimensions of Jesus' leadership — and open to His unconditional love in your life — you can come to lead like Jesus, which will make you a better leader in any context.

The person who wants to build his or her life around Christian principles today faces a challenge. Our society is increasingly secular.

A clear majority of us consider ourselves Christian. But we sense that it is not appropriate to mention Jesus — not even God — in the workplace or public square. If you are uncomfortable talking about God, Jesus, or your Christian faith in public, I've got great news for you: Leading like Jesus is not about what you say, but about *what you do.*

As you master what it means to lead like Jesus, some people may ask you about the source of your leadership aptitude. If they do, consider it an invitation to share your Christian leadership perspective. Since they have been impressed with how you lead and the results generated by your leadership, what you say will have real power to influence them. But until then, leading like Jesus is about what you *do* much more than what you say.

I therefore, the prisoner in the Lord, beg you to lead a life worthy of the calling to which you have been called, with all humility and gentleness, with patience, bearing with one another in love, making every effort to maintain the unity of the Spirit in the bond of peace.

EPHESIANS 4:1-3

"Only if we live in the right way, with one another and for one another, can freedom develop. . . . If we live in opposition to love and against the truth — in opposition to God — then we destroy one another and destroy the world." [2]

POPE BENEDICT XVI

"When we dream alone, we only dream. When we dream together, reality begins."

BRAZILIAN PROVERB

Chapter One

Catholicism's Two Leadership Challenges

Catholics face two particular leadership challenges. One chiefly concerns the laity. The other primarily concerns the clergy. But in today's Catholic community, both affect everyone.

With regard to the laity, a huge demographic transformation has had a profound effect on the challenges we face trying to live each day as faithful Christians. In the last half century, the Catholic Church in the United States has seen itself transformed from a church of the urban working poor to a church whose members are leaders in all sectors of society. Catholics make up about 24 percent of the nation's population. But it's estimated that Catholics make up as much as 40 percent of the nation's white collar population. The Catholic challenge today has changed from *how to fit into society* to *how to lead it*. We struggle with this challenge because it is a new one and we don't have a lot of models to guide us. Until recently, the only leadership experience most Catholics had in American culture was in our families. (For that reason, we will frequently draw on examples from family life to illustrate what it means to lead like Jesus in every walk of life.)

Our Church hasn't helped the laity much with their leadership challenge either. Catholic parishes are often well-equipped to gather their members for worship, dispense the sacraments, help those at the margins of society, and provide social outlets for members who were once shut out of society's mainstream. But helping members learn how to integrate their Christian faith with their lives as leaders at home, at work, and in their communities is a new challenge. Catholics don't hear much about it from the pulpit or in their media. This book represents an early step in helping Catholic laity integrate their faith with their lives in the 21st century.

With regard to our clergy (a term that includes bishops, priests, and permanent deacons), the Catholic Church is home to an interesting paradox. No organization spends more of its key resources — time and money— to educate its primary leaders. We require them to study for years and years before they are ordained. And yet, in most cases, none of their education deals with developing leadership skills. In the past, it was thought that diocesan priests, in particular, would get their leadership education on the job, while they served extended apprenticeships as associates to pastors in various parishes over the course of many years. Today, with the number of priestly vocations and ordinations down, diocesan priests are thrust into the pastor's role much sooner, often after only one or two experiences as an associate.

If we want consistently effective parish leaders, we will have to grow them. And yes, we certainly want better parish leaders. On the one hand, the leadership expectations of lay parishioners continue to rise with the level of their education and the broad experience their mobility gives them in a multitude of parish settings. On the other hand, their clerical leaders come to the leadership task with less experience than ever. No wonder many parishioners are disappointed, even frustrated, and let their enthusiasm wane — while many priests feel overwhelmed by the expectations and practical demands of their pastoral ministry.

It doesn't have to be this way — neither for the clergy nor for the laity. Jesus has an answer for our leadership challenges at work, at home, in our communities, and even in our parishes and church ministries. It is a simple answer. But it is not an easy one. Even so, it is within the grasp of every Christian who does his or her best to lead as Jesus calls us to lead and who asks for Jesus' help every day along the way.

This book is designed to outline the path that Jesus has cleared for us. It is my hope that it will help clergy and laity alike address the pressing need for better leadership in the Church and in the world.

─────────────── IN THE CHURCH ───────────────

Profile of a Servant Leader

A few years ago I met a priest after he moved into a parish where I am not a member but where I worship often. He had been serving in the parish for a month or two when I first encountered him at Mass. He was bald-headed and looked to be in his late 50s or early 60s, so I assumed he had a lot of experience as a priest. It was evident immediately that the parishioners had great affection for him. He was not an especially polished speaker, but his homilies were very down-to-earth, provided some practical insight, and always showed how much he loved God and cared for the people.

After just a few visits over a couple of months' time, it was clear that he was breathing new life into the parish. The parish was doing more — and doing it better, with more participation — than it had done in the past. After Mass, at the back of church, people stood in line to visit with him. He made a point to thank everyone for attending, giving special attention to children and teens. I was impressed with him, but even more with the reception his parishioners gave him. A couple of months later he mentioned that he would be celebrating the anniversary of his priestly ordination. I assumed it would be his 20th or 25th. Instead it was his first. Already impressed with his leadership skills, I was amazed that they could be so well-honed after just one year of priesthood.

A few weeks later he began his homily by asking the people to pray for the parishioners in a nearby town. Then he explained that he would be going there as pastor. The people were stunned. Several shouted, "Oh, no!"

A few weeks later I returned to the church. After reading the Gospel, the priest began to talk about how difficult it is to be a bishop. He said that a bishop's job is not made easier when he is besieged by phone calls, letters, and petitions. Obviously, the parishioners had rebelled against the priest's transfer. Now, although the priest didn't want to leave the parish, he defended the bishop's action.

The priest spoke of the pledge he made at ordination to obey his bishop. He told the people that he loved them and that he didn't want to leave them. But he added that part of being a priest is deferring to the bishop regarding the needs of the diocese — and that part of being laity is doing the same thing. He provided a few particulars about the difficult job their bishop had assigning priests to serve all the people in a time of great shortage. Then he asked the people to love, trust, and pray for their bishop and for him. After Mass, there were a lot of hugs and expressions of gratitude all around. The priest had won peace for his bishop and for his people.

I was more impressed than ever with this priest's powerful leadership skills and wondered about their source. So I asked to visit with him about his priesthood, and he agreed. Eventually, we sat down in the rectory of his new parish, and I asked where he learned to lead. I was not prepared for his answer.

"What I know about being a leader I learned as a Marine officer in Vietnam," he said. He explained that leading men in combat is not what it's depicted to be in the movies. It wasn't about yelling or throwing men at machine guns. He had a mission to accomplish, but he also had responsibility for the lives of the men in his command. As a leader, he could never forget either obligation.

After serving in the Marine Corps, he went on to build very successful computer services and software businesses using the leadership skills he had learned in combat. Eventually, one of these businesses supported him in the seminary (until he sold it).

He added that while he was in the seminary he was assigned every weekend to a parish with a pastor who was a wonderful mentor. With the pastor's guidance, he was able to refine the skills he had learned as a combat officer and honed as an entrepreneur to fit the needs of a parish. As we talked, attention turned to his new parish. It was already a lively place with a lot of parishioner involvement, but it was struggling financially. Still, he was confident that it could become better. He had met the people and quickly come to care for them. Together, in loving concern for one another, they could meet the challenge and overcome it. He already had a clear vision of an active, self-sustaining parish and was focused on serving the people's individual and collective needs so that the vision would become a reality.

I saw him again a year later. Again he told his parishioners he was being moved to another parish. It was his third parish in a little more than two years. Some of the boxes he had moved into the rectory a year ago were still waiting to be unpacked. My guess is that his bishop would like to clone him. But since that's not possible, he's doing the next best thing: he's putting this priest in as many places as he can, hoping his leadership skills ignite more and more people to become more effective leaders themselves.

The cynic would say, "No good deed goes unpunished." And, in truth, the frequent moves were beginning to wear on the man. But he knew what it meant to be a priest, and he had accepted the stole freely, despite great personal sacrifice. He was called, and he would follow . . . again and again.

When he was ordained, this man was ready to be an exceptionally effective parish leader — and the people noticed it instantly. In his case, we have the U.S. Marine Corps and a gifted, dedicated mentor to thank for his incredible pastoral leadership skills. But we can't rely on the Department of Defense to train all our pastors for effective leadership. If we want truly powerful leaders in the Church — people who can enkindle and enrich the faith of the laity — we will have to equip them to lead like Jesus.

REFLECTION QUESTIONS

- Do I ever experience difficulty applying my faith convictions to the situations that arise in my everyday life?
- If so, when and where does this happen most often? In what roles do I experience the most difficulty? Why is this so?
- What is the greatest challenge I currently face as I try to live my faith and function as a leader at home, at work, in my community, or in my parish?
- Do I sometimes look for faith guidance in fulfilling my various roles in life and not find it? In which roles does this happen most often? Why do I think that's true?
- Who are the people most directly impacted by my leadership thinking and behavior? What do I most want for each of them?

"Go therefore and make disciples of all nations, baptizing them in the name of the Father and of the Son and of the Holy Spirit, and teaching them to obey everything that I have commanded you. And remember, I am with you always, to the end of the age."

MATTHEW 28:19-20

"It is to all Christians that we address a fresh and insistent call to action. In our encyclical on the Development of Peoples we urged that all should set themselves to the task: 'Laymen should take up as their own proper task the renewal of the temporal order. . . . It belongs to the laity, without waiting passively for orders and directives, to take the initiative freely and to infuse a Christian spirit into the mentality, customs, laws and structures of the community in which they live.'"[3]

POPE PAUL VI

Chapter Two

What Is Our Purpose?

L ay Catholics of a certain age grew up thinking their purpose in the Church, and perhaps in life, was to "pray, pay, and obey." However, Jesus had a much larger role in mind for us. So did many of our Church leaders down through the ages. We might not have heard about their vision for us in childhood catechism classes because it concerns how we function as adults. But since we are now adults, we should consider it.

At Vatican II, the council fathers addressed this issue as soon as they addressed the meaning of baptism. Quoting 1 Peter 2:9, they wrote that baptism makes us part of Jesus' own body and consecrates us "into a kingly priesthood and a holy nation" where we are called to "witness to Christ all the world over."[4] Makes us sound important, doesn't it? But perhaps it also sounds a little too idealistic to fit the reality of our everyday lives. Elsewhere in the documents of Vatican II, the council fathers offered a more down-to-earth description of the role of all baptized persons:

> By reason of their special vocation it belongs to the laity to seek the kingdom of God by engaging in temporal affairs and directing them according to God's will. They live in the world, that is, they are engaged in each and every work and business of the earth and in the ordinary circumstances of social and family life which, as it were, constitute their very existence. There they are called by God that, being led by the spirit to the Gospel, they may contribute to the sanctification of the world, as from within like leaven, by fulfilling their own particular duties. Thus, especially by the witness of their life, resplendent in faith, hope and charity they must manifest Christ to others. It pertains to them in a special way so to illuminate and order all temporal things with which they are so

closely associated that these may be effected and grow according to Christ and may be to the glory of the Creator and Redeemer.[5]

Here we are presented with a clear call to lead like Jesus in our everyday lives at home, at work, and in our communities. To summarize:

- **What are the laity called by Christ to do?** To work for the "sanctification of the world."
- **How are we to do it?** By "the witness of [our] life, resplendent in faith, hope and charity." (Clearly, it is much more a matter of what we do than what we say.)

A few years after the Second Vatican Council ended, Pope Paul VI added a note of urgency regarding the laity's special mission in the world. He issued an "insistent call to action" for us to "infuse a Christian spirit" into the world around us — noting that we should not wait passively "for orders and directives."[6]

What Is Sanctification?

If the vocation of every baptized Catholic is to "sanctify the world," it's only fair to ask: What is sanctification? Perhaps the best definition is found in Vatican II's call "to infuse the Christian spirit into the mentality and behavior, laws and structures of the community in which one lives."[7] This isn't the only time we've been told that it's our job. Pope John Paul II said basically the same thing to lay people when he visited the United States in 1987:

> As lay men and women actively engaged in this temporal order, you are being called by Christ to sanctify the world and to transform it. This is true of *all work, however exalted or humble*, but it is especially urgent for those whom circumstances and special talent have placed in positions of leadership or influence: men and women in public service, education, business, science, social communications, and the arts.[8]

Notice that the pope said that the call "to sanctify the world and to transform it" applies to "all work, however exalted or humble."

A Warning About Preaching

"Be sure that you first preach by the way you live. If you do not, people will notice that you say one thing, but live otherwise, and your words will bring only cynical laughter and a derisive shake of the head."

St. Charles Borromeo

But obviously, he was also aware of what had happened to American Catholics as a people since the end of World War II. Thanks to the GI Bill and a booming economy, in one generation Catholicism in the United States moved from a church of the urban working poor to a church of suburban, upper-middle-class leaders and managers. So the pope said that the work of sanctifying and transforming the world is "especially urgent for those whom circumstances and special talent have placed in positions of leadership or influence."

Clearly, all of us who are baptized share a calling to "sanctify the world." It's "especially urgent" that those of us with leadership positions in the world respond to that calling. But if we conclude that this calling is limited only to our roles in the work world, we miss the point entirely. A poster that was popular a few decades ago got it exactly right: "Bloom where you are planted." As Church leaders have consistently made clear over the ages, our vocation to sanctify the world involves all our roles — and most especially those of spouse, parent, and citizen.

In his remarks to some U.S. bishops on their *ad limina* visits to Rome on May 28, 2004, Pope John Paul II put it this way:

> Now is above all the hour of the lay faithful, who, by their specific vocation to shape the secular world in accordance with the Gospel, are called to carry forward the Church's prophetic mission by evangelizing the various spheres of family, social, professional and cultural life.

Did He Say "Evangelizing"?

Many lay Catholics are not used to hearing the words "evangelizing" and "evangelization." Even less are we accustomed to hearing that our role is to "evangelize" anyone. But the pope whom many call *Pope John Paul the Great* said that the laity's responsibility includes "evangelizing." Like it or not, he deserves a fair hearing.

Many of us associate "evangelizing" with something freelance preachers once did on street corners and under tents, but now do on television and radio. If evangelizing is preaching, most Catholics are pretty sure they want nothing to do with it. We're relieved to learn that preaching is a job that's reserved for bishops, priests, and deacons, and we're only too happy to let them do it — unless, of course, they drone on for very long.

But if we aren't expected to preach, how can we be expected to evangelize? When Pope John Paul II, his predecessors, and his successor talk about evangelization, they have in mind something much broader — and frankly, with more lasting impact — than standing on a street corner, in a pulpit, or on a stage preaching. Instead, their perspective recalls the advice of St. Francis of Assisi, who told his followers, "Go and preach the Gospel, and if you must, use words."

IN THE FAMILY

Prove It to Yourself in Just a Minute

To confirm that actions speak louder than words, try a little experiment. It takes just a minute. During this minute you should close your eyes, sit back, and relax. But first, read the next paragraph.

✦ **Here's how to spend your minute:** Think about your relationship with your parent who has had the greatest influence on your life. If both have had an equal influence, pick one arbitrarily. Imagine yourself with that parent. Where are you? What are you doing? Mentally envision the scene. What do you notice? Describe the sights, smells, and sounds. What do you remember most about this parent? What do you appreciate most? What really stands out? Think about his or her lasting impact on you. What matters most about him or her?

✦ **Now close your eyes for about a minute and begin the exercise.** You can have someone time you, set a timer, or just estimate the time. When you are done, open your eyes and read the next paragraph.

✦ **Now ask yourself:** *Was I thinking about things my parent said to me or things my parent did? Did I recall things he or she told me or the sacrifices that were made, the cheerfulness that was displayed, the affection that was shared, the focus he or she had, the pies or cookies that were baked, the love that was given me, the confidence he or she showed in me?* After you have thought about this, read on.

I have been conducting this experiment for years, and except for two very special cases, the answer has always been the same: *We remember what our parents did.* We remember how they lived.

Isn't that surprising? After all, good parents are giving directions constantly. "Do this! Don't to that! Yada, yada, yada." Yet what sticks and continues to shape our lives long after our parents are gone is not so much what they said, but what they did. (In fact, if what they said contradicted what they did, we rejected their advice as hypocritical.)

If you are a parent who fears that your children don't listen to a thing you say, this new awareness may give you some consolation and reason to hope for the future. It's not your words so much as your deeds that matter to your children.

Of course, if your behavior needs improvement, there's no better time to work on it than right now — before it does further harm shaping your children's long-term development.

Words are important. We use them to share the meaning of events with one another. But we've always known that *deeds speak louder than words*, especially when it comes to shaping human lives.

Our Greatest Power

Our greatest power to have lasting influence on the people around us is rooted in our everyday behavior, not in the words we use to tell others what to do. That's true in all our relationships. And that's how we can evangelize (or scandalize) without using words. In fact, that's how we can sometimes evangelize (or scandalize) without even being aware of what we are doing.

For all Christians (including clergy, but most especially for lay Christians), evangelization is not nearly so much about *talking the talk* as it is about *walking the walk*. Of course, this has always been true. Way back about A.D. 200, a priest and theologian by the name of Tertullian noted that the deeds of love among his fellow Christians had led non-Christians "to put a brand on us" — expressed in the phrase "see how they love one another."[9] That had to be particularly gratifying to Christians of that time because their leader, Jesus, had told them: "I give you a new commandment, that you love one another. Just as I have loved you, you also should love one another" (Jn 13:34).

IN THE CHURCH

Everyday Actions Influence Hundreds of Thousands

It's clear that actions speak louder than words — and that we evangelize without words — when we look at the success of the Rite of Christian Initiation of Adults (RCIA) in our Church. Every year thousands of adults freely join the Church after a long process of study, reflection, and discussion in parish RCIA programs.

What got them started down this path to becoming Catholic?

Over the years I've had a chance to talk with many of them, and I always like to ask them what drew them to the Church. Many are drawn to the Church by a spouse or other family member, which speaks of the power that our close relationships have to shape our lives and even, on occasion, turn them in a new direction. Nearly always, the others I meet who have gone through the RCIA process share stories about the impact a Catholic friend or neighbor had on them in the course of their everyday lives. Here are the kinds of things I hear:

+ "They just seemed to have their act together."
+ "They were such a healthy, happy family."

- ✦ "They were so nice to us when we moved in, and kept on being nice."
- ✦ "The woman next door checked in on me when I was ill."
- ✦ "The man down the street was always pleasant. When my lawnmower broke, he came over and cut my grass."
- ✦ "They just seemed to have something I was missing."
- ✦ "I wanted to be more like them."
- ✦ "I wanted to have what I saw they had."

Typically, they will add: "At some point we just started talking." So yes, words are important. But nearly always the seed is planted when someone notices that a lay Catholic person, couple, or family seems to be endowed with something that makes them a little happier or considerate. Their lives seem more purposeful or satisfying.

It's what we do that matters most. In fact, it's what we do that prompts others to inquire about what we have to say. Only when our lives reflect a Christian dimension do our words have the power to attract instead of to repel.

As we consider our individual and collective purpose as Christians today — and our impact on the world — we have to ask ourselves several questions:

- Is love still Christianity's primary "brand" today?
- If not, why not?
- Is our love the first thing that others notice about us as Christians?
- Or are there other things in our behavior that brand us in other ways? (Gandhi once observed: "I like your Christ. I do not like your Christians. Your Christians are so unlike your Christ. If Christians really lived according to the teachings of Christ, as found in the Bible, all of India would be Christian today." At another time, he was reputedly asked if he would ever consider being a Christian. He said he would if he could find one.)

- What can I do to make that brand — *how Christians love one another* — the hallmark of my faith as people see me living it?

When we talk about being Christian but then don't live consistently with our profession of faith, we drive people away from Christianity. It turns out that some people leave the Church for much the same reason that other people come to the Church: *the behavior of Church members.*

I served for many years as a Church spokesman in the media, so I am publicly associated with Christianity. That role provided me with many opportunities to meet people who have abandoned church participation. I'm always willing to listen to their stories, and in nearly every case it turns out that they don't go to church at least in part because of someone who does. That tells us Christians that *how we act* shapes the brand that Christianity has in people's hearts and minds today.

This is a particular burden for clergy because they can almost never escape being associated with the Church. Everything they are seen doing and saying reflects on people's view of Christianity, and often people expect them to be perfect. But it is a burden for the rest of us, too. Whenever anyone knows we are Christian, whatever we do and whatever we fail to do can reflect on all Christians and on Christianity itself. Perhaps that's why many of us are happy to leave all talk of religion outside of the public arena, especially outside our place of work, and why some of us even drift away from religious practice. If no one knows we're Christian, at least we can't be accused of giving Christianity a bad name.

But Jesus set the bar higher than that. He says our role is to live in such a way that we help the Gospel take root everywhere. Catholic bishops in the United States affirmed Jesus' teaching in their 1998 pastoral letter *Everyday Christianity: To Hunger and Thirst for Justice*:

> Followers of the Lord Jesus live their discipleship as spouses and parents, single adults and youth, employers and employees, consumers and investors, citizens and neighbors. We renew the warning of the Second Vatican Council that the "split between the faith

which many profess and their daily lives deserves to be counted among the more serious errors of our age." By our Baptism and Confirmation every member of our community is called to live his or her faith in the world.

Many of us hunger to integrate our faith with our everyday lives. We want to avoid the unfortunate split between faith and life mentioned by the council fathers and the nation's bishops. Fortunately, we are given a good place to start with the opportunity to learn to lead like Jesus.

REFLECTION QUESTIONS

- Does my everyday behavior contribute to my purpose as a Christian to sanctify the world?
- Where and where not?
- Why or why not?
- What might I do in one of my relationships or in one of my roles to help sanctify the world?

David consulted with the commanders of the thousands and of the hundreds, with every leader. David said to the whole assembly of Israel, "If it seems good to you, and if it is the will of the LORD our God, let us send abroad to our kindred who remain in all the land of Israel, including the priests and Levites in the cities that have pasture lands, that they may come together to us. Then let us bring again the ark of our God to us; for we did not turn to it in the days of Saul." The whole assembly agreed to do so, for the thing pleased all the people.

1 CHRONICLES 13:1-4

"From everyone to whom much has been given, much will be required; and from the one to whom much has been entrusted, even more will be demanded."

LUKE 12:48

"Life is no brief candle to me. It is a sort of splendid torch which I have got a hold of for the moment, and I want to make it burn as brightly as possible before handing it on to future generations."

GEORGE BERNARD SHAW

Chapter Three

Who Is a Leader?

Everyone is a leader. It's a role no one can completely escape. As my colleagues Ken Blanchard and Phil Hodges say in *Lead Like Jesus: Lessons from the Greatest Role Model of All Time,* "Leadership is a process of influence."[10] Whenever you seek to influence another person, you are taking on the role of a leader.

In fact, sometimes you are leading when you are not even aware of it. A famous athlete once insisted that he was not a role model for children; he was just a basketball player. Commentators scoffed. They told him, "It's not your call." When someone observes your behavior and imitates it, you are a leader whether you like it or not. If children decide to imitate someone, that person is serving in a leadership role even if he or she isn't aware of it. That's true for athletes, entertainers, and other prominent people. But it's even truer for parents and other family members, family friends, local community figures, and teachers. If you doubt this, take the quiz featured in the "In the Community" section on the next page.

Children imitate the adults around them — especially their parents — without even thinking about it. If parents try to do their best, their children benefit from their modeling as much as from their nurturing. But if parents don't care how their behavior influences their children, then the odds decline that their children will benefit from how the parents behave. Of course, parents aren't the only models we find in life. As we grow, we continue to model the behaviors of other people we admire. In this way, people often have deeper, more profound leadership impacts than they ever know. But certainly all of us are leaders at some times and some places in our lives.

Gratifying and Humbling Lessons in Leadership

The fact that we are all leaders at some points in our lives — sometimes even when we are not aware of it — was brought home to me in a gratifying yet humbling way as I approached my 60th birthday. A note arrived in the mail from a woman who lived in a town we had moved away from more than 30 years before. In that town I worked for a newspaper publishing company that had hired me while I was still in college. It was a small but rapidly growing newspaper publishing company, and we generally thought of ourselves as family. Looking back, I would have sworn I knew the first name of everyone on the payroll. But the note that arrived more than three decades later was from someone whose name I could not remember.

The woman wrote that she had just returned from a long trip and was blessed to have taken many beautiful photos that she would cherish. Whenever she looked at them, they could transport her back

---

IN THE COMMUNITY

Lasting Leadership Quiz: Who Matters Most?

It's easy for us to see how famous athletes, movie stars, and other celebrities appear to have an impact on people of all ages in our culture. We wear their expensive jerseys and shoes, adopt their expressions and fashions, imitate their grooming, buy their movies and music, and seemingly try to adopt their identities. This is especially true of young people.

So who are the role models who really shape our behavior long term? To find out, try this little quiz on yourself, your friends, and relatives and especially any teenagers in your home.

Part I: Answer the first six questions as well as you can.

1. Name the five richest people in the world.
2. Name the last five Heisman Trophy winners.
3. Name the last five winners of the Miss America Contest.
4. Name 10 people who have won the Nobel or Pulitzer Prize. How about five?

5. Name the last half dozen Academy Award winners for best actor and best actress.
6. Name the last decade's World Series winners.

How are you doing? Don't get discouraged. You may find the next ones easier.

Part II: Answer the next five questions as well as you can.

7. List a few teachers who aided your journey through school.
8. Name three friends who have helped you through a difficult time.
9. Name five people who have taught you something worthwhile.
10. Think of a few people who have made you feel appreciated and special.
11. Think of five people you enjoy spending time with.

A reflection: When it comes to having an impact and lasting influence on people, obviously it's not about position, money, or fame. Applause dies. Awards tarnish. Achievements are forgotten. Titles slip away. The paparazzi disappear. Lasting influence comes with intimacy: we are most influenced by the people we believe care most about us.

---

to enjoy again her wonderful adventure. She said that for many years she had meant to write, but finally she could no longer put it off. She wanted me to know how grateful she was for having inspired her interest in photography, which had enriched her life in so many ways for so many years. To my chagrin and shame, I could not remember this woman at all. To this day, I have no recollection of the role I played in a life-changing experience for her. Although I am embarrassed by my faulty memory, I am grateful that she wrote — and for reminding me of how our actions can serve a leadership purpose even when we are not remotely aware of it.

A more dramatic story is one told to me about a poor governess' global legacy. Some years ago I met a Hindu from India who was beginning to make his mark as a real estate developer in the United States and soon would become a multimillionaire. At the time, I was looking for investors to launch a Catholic publication. One of my brothers worked with this man and told me that he might be interested in my project. I was skeptical that a Hindu would want to invest in a Catholic publication, but I trusted my brother's judgment and made an appointment to visit the man.

He received me graciously and quickly confirmed his interest. I couldn't help asking him why he would want to invest in an explicitly Catholic product. He told me the story of a governess who practically raised him as a boy in India. She was a wonderful woman for whom he felt the deepest gratitude. It also happened that she was Catholic

―――――――――――IN THE FAMILY―――――――――――

The Power to Shape Lives

We are all always educators because people are always observing our behavior. What we do influences people much more than what we say. This is especially true in the parent-child relationship, as the following poem makes clear. The author says her reflections were inspired by her mother.

When You Thought I Wasn't Looking[11]
By Mary Rita Schilke Korzan

When you thought I wasn't looking
You hung my first painting on the refrigerator
And I wanted to paint another.

When you thought I wasn't looking
You fed a stray cat
And I thought it was good to be kind to animals.

When you thought I wasn't looking
You baked a birthday cake just for me
And I knew that little things were special things.

When you thought I wasn't looking
You said a prayer

And I believed there was a God that
   I could always talk to.

When you thought I wasn't looking
You kissed me good-night
And I felt loved.

When you thought I wasn't looking
I saw tears come from your eyes
And I learned that sometimes things hurt —
   But that it's alright to cry.

When you thought I wasn't looking
You smiled
And it made me want to look that pretty too.

When you thought I wasn't looking
You cared
And I wanted to be everything I could be.

When you thought I wasn't looking —
I looked . . .
And wanted to say thanks
For all those things you did
When you thought I wasn't looking.

---

and faithfully attended Mass every Sunday. On occasion, she would take him along, and he was intrigued by the ritual. Although she was paid only a relative pittance, she always found a way to buy him birthday and holiday presents, something not expected of servants. In addition to her remarkable care and contributions to his development, he was impressed by her kindness and generosity.

Eventually, she died, and he attended the funeral. That's when he learned it had always been her heart's desire to be a nun, but she hadn't joined a religious order because she felt an obligation to help support her family. Instead, she decided to live as a celibate governess and to send nearly all of her small stipend home to her family, living elsewhere in India. Hers had been a life of totally selfless service.

That realization overwhelmed him. He also recognized that the gifts she had bought him were purchased with funds she could have sent home to help her needy family. The thought that his happiness mattered so much to her was almost more than he could bear.

In India, a land where religious tolerance has sometimes been a struggle and where Christians are just a tiny minority of the population, a poor and seemingly powerless governess imbued a young Hindu man with an appreciation for Christianity in general and a deep regard for Catholics in particular. He said he wanted to invest in my Catholic enterprise for two reasons: it appeared to be an attractive risk/reward opportunity and it would honor his boyhood governess. He wrote a check for a substantial number of shares and slid it across the table to me.

Who would say that this poor, obscure woman was not a leader? Indeed, her leadership was so powerful that it continued to exert an influence many years after she had gone to her grave. St. Francis of Assisi would have appreciated her sublime leadership contribution because she lived fully Francis' admonition to preach the Gospel without words. Because of that, the force of her deeds still resonates decades later halfway around the world. In her own humble way, truly she was a leader in the image of Jesus.

This devoted servant's example reminds us that there are two realms of leadership: *life role* and *organizational*.

- *Organizational leadership* gets more attention in our mass culture. CEOs of big companies are celebrities — either for the billions of dollars they generate and the shareholders they enrich, or for the billions of dollars they squander and the lives they destroy, sometimes by breaking the law. The public is fascinated by these stories of the rich, famous, and powerful.
- But I'm convinced that *life-role leadership* is the more important of the two. Over the years, I've held a number of prominent leadership roles: editor, publisher, vice president of a large business, business owner, and college professor. But all of them pale in importance to my role as a husband and father because no outcomes are more important to me than the lives

of my wife and children. More than anything else in the world I want to make a positive contribution to their development and well-being.

All of us are leaders of one sort or another at various times in our lives. But not all of us are effective leaders. Effective leadership involves a few key attributes that the Lead Like Jesus movement wants to share with the whole world, and the *S³ Leadership Framework* is a fine way to understand what it means to lead like Jesus. When we employ the *S³ Leadership Framework* to try to lead like Jesus, we open the door to incredible growth and development in ourselves and in all of the persons and organizations with whom we interact.

The journey begins by recognizing that effective long-term leadership begins inside us. It is a matter of character. We cannot give what we do not have. Inevitably, leadership moments come to us in this life. What we do with them is largely a matter of the choices we have made up to that point about the person we want to be and the legacy we want to leave. Ultimately, effective leadership is not about formal power or money. It is about integrity. Leadership begins in the heart. Jesus tells us we need to have the heart of a servant.

Understanding Power

When some people hear the phrase "leading like Jesus," they are reluctant to listen because they think of Jesus as a "nice guy" and a "softie" who might not be able to cut it in today's competitive world. Leadership, they believe, is about power. Effective leaders are strong people who are forceful and willing to bully and punish others to get compliance. Jesus' leadership was nothing like that. But neither was it "soft." In fact, it was very demanding. Despite Jesus' gentleness, He was able to attract followers who would eventually die for Him because He had wisdom about the roots of real, lasting power that modern researchers are only beginning to understand.

Let's take a closer look at the five bases for power, as outlined by John French and Bertram Raven,[12] to see why they are not equal. They are:

1. **Reward power** — the ability to give rewards and grant favors.
2. **Coercive power** — the ability to threaten and apply punishment.
3. **Legitimate (or official) power** — the ability to direct others' behavior by virtue of one's formal position.
4. **Expert power** — the ability to influence people because you know more than others or you have access to information that others don't have.
5. **Referent power** — also called charisma or role model power, the ability to influence people because they perceive that you somehow deserve to be followed, perhaps because they believe you will achieve group success that others cannot or because they believe you care about them.

Which Powers Are the Most Powerful?

The first three types are the ones most commonly associated with power. Yet, studies show that the fourth and fifth types are more powerful when it comes to having a lasting influence on people.

The power to reward (1) and legitimate or official power (3) are only slightly effective when it comes to influencing others' behavior long term, and coercive power (2) actually has a negative correlation on influencing long-term behavior. Apparently, when we rely on threats or punishment in an effort to shape others' behavior, over the long term we will encounter more resistance than compliance.

The Limits of Official Power

Although we are sometimes tempted to think that official power should be the strongest, a telling example of the limits of official power came when President Richard Nixon, under siege for having lied about initiating the Watergate break-in, appeared on TV to defend himself and proclaimed, "I am the president!" It probably marked the U.S. presidency's weakest moment in the 20th century. People mocked him. In short order, Nixon, facing impeachment, was forced to resign from the office.

Where Do the Powers Come From?

It's important to understand where these different types of power come from. The first three sources, the weaker ones, originate in the environment. For instance, a parent's power is rooted in biology and a social structure; a boss' power is rooted in an organizational structure. In both of these examples, the leaders have an official position of authority that also gives them the powers to reward and punish.

In contrast, the last two types of power, which are the most powerful types, originate in the relationship of leader and follower. Expert power arises not simply because a leader has expertise, but also because the follower recognizes that expertise. The final type of power, referent power, is actually given to the leader by the follower. This type of power can be extraordinarily effective for both good and bad. A tragic example of such power gone awry is the Jonestown cult in which the followers of Jim Jones willingly followed him in a mass suicide in 1978.

—————IN THE CHURCH—————

The Power of a Priest

During a recent Lent, a friend wrote to me about the power her pastor was exercising in her life:

> Our pastor has challenged all of us to get into spring training now that the Super Bowl is over. We have six weeks to prepare for the big day, which of course is Easter. He told us to make our own training work schedule, which should include prayer, sacrifice, and service. What a great analogy! I have to admit that having him state it so simply for us who are simple-minded was effective. I really like his humble, gentle spirit. His presence and his words command attention and always have me leaving church reflecting on his message. He is so good. I wonder how we will keep him. He is not charismatic, but his gentle, challenging love of the Lord and Church and sacraments is always present.

Of course, the priest's official power put him in the pulpit. But clearly, it's "his humble, gentle spirit" and his "gentle, challenging love" that are the sources of the power he has to influence people long after they have left his presence. His spirit prompts people to be moved by his words and to share them with others near and far. In fact, it's for that very reason you are reading about him now. This kind of power does not come by virtue of his official position or his ordination, but by virtue of the relationship he has cultivated with his parishioners and the power they have decided to give him in their lives.

REFLECTION QUESTIONS

- Who have been the leaders in my life?
- For what am I most indebted to them? Was it things they said or things they did?
- Has anyone served as a leader in my life who wasn't aware of his or her leadership role? How did he or she influence me?
- Who might regard me as a leader to follow? What kind of example am I for him or her?

"The greatest among you will be your servant. All who exalt themselves will be humbled, and all who humble themselves will be exalted."

MATTHEW 23:11-12

"By this everyone will know that you are my disciples, if you have love for one another."

JOHN 13:35

Chapter Four

S¹: Called to Be a Servant Leader —
The Leadership of Jesus

What Servant Leadership Is NOT

Before we investigate what it means to be a *servant leader*, let us begin by noting what servant leadership is not. It is not about structure. In fact, servant leadership can thrive in any structure. Take the case of Jesus' own leadership.

Jesus did not build a complex organization. He did not install a great many levels of decision making in His organization. Clearly, He had an inner circle: the apostles. He spent more time with this group than with His other disciples, teaching them how to understand His mission and how to lead others. Near the end of His ministry He also picked one of his apostles, Peter, to lead His followers when He was gone. But if we look at how Jesus' organization behaved while He was here on earth, we see that Jesus called all the shots. He did not gather His apostles and ask, "Now that we're all here together, what do you think we should do? What is our mission?" Instead, Jesus provided the mission. He provided the direction. Jesus made all the decisions. The political term for an organization like that is an *autocracy*. So Jesus, in a political sense, was an *autocrat*. Yet, He was also the model *servant leader*.

How can that be? It's possible to be both an autocrat and a servant leader because servant leadership is not about structure. It is about *relationships*. Long before Jesus walked the earth, the Greek philosopher Plato developed the concept of "philosopher-kings," leaders who would devote their lives to becoming "in every way best at everything," and yet were willing to submit to "the good itself" and to share power with one another. Plato speaks of leaders who are humble and

45

A Bishop-Saint Explains His Role

"For you I am a bishop, but with you I am a Christian. The first is an office accepted; the second is a gift received. One is danger; the other is safety. If I am happier to be redeemed with you than to be placed over you, then I shall, as the Lord commanded, be more fully your servant."[13]

ST. AUGUSTINE OF HIPPO

---

focused on their mission rather than on their own good. The notion of "benign despot" also points to leaders whose powers may be absolute in a political or practical sense, but who exercise their power for the sake of the governed rather than for their own sakes, and so they are servant leaders.

Although Americans generally don't like kings, despots, or autocrats, we do tend to associate leadership with having some sort of formal position and title. But the power to influence people on a lasting basis has more to do with how we relate to people than with any positions or titles we hold. Jesus' own leadership example confirms this. In the Gospel of Matthew, we find the account of Jesus telling a crowd the parable of the foolish man who built his house on sand and the wise man who built his house on rock. We read that "the crowds were astounded at his teaching, for he taught them as one having authority, and not as their scribes" (Mt 7:28-29).

The scribes had formal authority, but obviously they did not exercise a strong influence on people. Jesus had no formal authority, and yet He had such powerful effect on people that they decided to follow Him. The kind of power and influence — *leadership* — that Jesus exhibited sounds very much like the two most powerful sources of power mentioned earlier: expert power and referent power. The people recognized a special wisdom in the words of Jesus, and they decided that what He said and did made Him a worthy leader for them to follow. As Jesus' impact on others illustrated, the powerful, lasting leadership that is characteristic of true servant leadership is not about structure; it is about *relationships*.

So how does one go about becoming a servant leader?

The Most Important Things

Imagine that you know you are going to die tomorrow. You have invited your closest friends to share a last meal with you tonight. What will you talk about? The weather? The stock market's performance? The prospects for your favorite team? If your friends don't know this is the last time you will be with them before you die, they might show up expecting to talk about such mundane topics. But tonight is different. Tonight you want to focus on the things that are *most important* in your life.

Would it have been any different for Jesus at the Last Supper? Surely what He said and did at the Last Supper focused on those things that were most important to Him. Here's a brief list of His priorities, drawn from all four Gospels:

- Institutes the Eucharist (Mt 26; Mk 14; Lk 22)
- Endures Judas' betrayal (Mt 26; Mk 14; Lk 22; Jn 13, 18)
- Foretells Peter's denial (Mt 26; Mk 14; Lk 22; Jn 13)
- Hears an argument about who the greatest is (Lk 22)
- Instructs disciples how to lead (Lk 22; Jn 13)
- Models servant leadership — washes feet (Jn 13)
- Gives disciples the commandment to love (Jn 13)

Whenever I ask a group of Catholics what happened at the Last Supper, they are sure to mention that Jesus instituted the Eucharist. They nearly always note that Jesus washed His apostles' feet, and they often mention most of the other things on the list. But they seldom recall *why* Jesus said He washed the feet of His disciples and almost never mention that He instructed His apostles *how* to lead.

Why don't we remember that Jesus chose to talk about leadership with His followers on the night before He died? My guess is that we have a hard time understanding how we can be servants and leaders at the same time. It goes against everything we've learned about leadership. So we just skim past His teaching without taking any note of it. But Jesus did tell us in very specific terms how to lead. In fact, it's mentioned in three of the Gospels and demonstrated in the fourth. And because both St. Luke and St. John tell us that Jesus brought up the topic at the Last Supper, we can assume that leadership — *how we should lead* — was a very important matter to Him.

Jesus as Model and Teacher

If how we should lead was important to Jesus, it should be important to us. So it's time to take a closer look at what Jesus taught and did as a leader. Let's begin by looking at what He said about leadership at the Last Supper:

> A dispute also arose among them as to which one of them was to be regarded as the greatest. But he said to them, "The kings of the Gentiles lord it over them; and those in authority over them are called benefactors. But not so with you; rather the greatest among

————— IN THE CHURCH —————

A Pope Prefers a Hug to a Bow

At the investiture ceremony when Cardinal Karol Wojtyla became Pope John Paul II, members of the College of Cardinals lined up to individually pledge their fidelity to him. The dean of the college came first. Ordinarily, the other cardinals would follow in order of seniority. Instead, the pope saw to it that the second cardinal in line was Stefan Wyszynski, the primate of his native Poland.

Precedent called for the cardinal to genuflect before the seated pope, but Pope John Paul II had another idea. According to George Weigel, in his book *Witness to Hope: The Biography of Pope John Paul II*, as the elderly cardinal started to genuflect, the pope "rose from his throne, bent down, seized the old man, and locked him in a long embrace."[14] As the pope showed by example, servant leaders are not bound by the trappings of authority but by the bonds of filial affection.

you must become like the youngest, and the leader like one who serves." (Lk 22:24-26)

In Matthew 20:25-28 and in Mark 10:42-44, we find Jesus saying virtually the same thing. Later, in the Gospel of St. Matthew, Jesus adds to His leadership lesson when He says: "The greatest among you will be your servant. All who exalt themselves will be humbled, and all who humble themselves will be exalted" (Mt 23:11-12). In the Gospel of St. Mark, Jesus tells His apostles much the same thing: "Whoever wants to be first must be last of all and servant of all" (Mk 9:35).

If after reading these accounts from three of the Gospels any doubt remains that Jesus believes leaders must be servants, He dispels it in the Gospel of St. John, where at the Last Supper He demonstrates His conviction by stooping to wash the feet of His disciples and then giving them an explanation for what He has done.

After He had washed their feet, put on His robe, and returned to the table, He said to them:

"Do you know what I have done to you? You call me Teacher and Lord — and you are right, for that is what I am. So if I, your Lord and Teacher, have washed your feet, you also ought to wash one another's feet. For I have set you an example, that you also should do as I have done to you." (Jn 13:12-15)

The Gospels make it clear that Jesus wants us — no, *expects* us — to be servant leaders.

Crazy or Brilliant? You Make the Call

For those of us brought up to think of leaders as powerful, forceful figures who dominate and intimidate others, Jesus' teaching can seem insane. We understand how a leader can be a *tyrant*. But how in God's name can a leader ever be a *servant*? Isn't that like letting students run the school or allowing prisoners to take over the prison? Most people associate effective leadership with establishing a dominating presence, enforcing rules, issuing orders, and making sure that others

> ## The Role of Priests
>
> *"The priesthood is not an institution that exists alongside the laity or above it. The priesthood of bishops and priests, as well as the ministry of deacons, is for the laity, and precisely for this reason it possesses a ministerial character, that is to say, one of service."*[15]
>
> POPE JOHN PAUL II

do what they're told. It's all about "command and control." Jesus seems to be turning all of that on its head.

And yet, we know from the Gospels that Jesus was certainly a dominating presence. He issued orders and enforced rules. When His disciples strayed from His direction — or didn't understand Him — He had no difficulty being direct. If we are to accept Jesus as our model leader, we have to acknowledge that being direct with people has a place in leadership. Nevertheless, it's also obvious in the Gospels that Jesus did not think that "lording over" people had a legitimate place in leadership. For Jesus, the core of leadership is being a *servant*.

It may surprise you to learn that modern scholarship supports Jesus' perspective on leadership. For example, Jim Collins, one of today's most influential and widely read experts on leadership, has studied hundreds of companies. He sums up the evidence he has uncovered about effective leadership in a model with five levels of effectiveness, the fifth level being considered the most effective:[16]

1. Highly Capable Individual
2. Contributing Team Member
3. Competent Manager
4. Effective Leader
5. Level 5 Executive

What distinguishes a Level 4 leader from a Level 5 leader? Collins says that the leader at the very top of the leadership pinnacle "builds enduring greatness through a paradoxical blend of personal humility and professional will."[17] His discoveries are all the more influential

A Humble Priest Becomes a Pope

In his book *Witness to Hope: The Biography of Pope John Paul II*, George Weigel describes the early priesthood of Karol Wojtyla, who later became Pope John Paul II: "He soon began to attract followers, who found his 'naturalness,' as one put it, an attractive alternative to the regime-cowed professors at the universities and to the more clerically minded and distant Polish priests they had previously known."

People were not put off by his humble dress, although many remember his worn cassocks and cheap shoes. As soon as he arrived at his new assignment, he began to visit student dormitories and boarding houses to build relationships with the students. Knowing he would have to engage the students intellectually, he soon "started a series of Thursday evening conferences on two basic issues: the existence of God and the spiritual character of the human person."

Weigel notes that Father Wojtyla's early sermons were "a bit heavy philosophically. But the young priest's openness to criticism soon led him to a more accessible speaking style." He had the humility to ask the people about the quality of his work and to take to heart what he heard. That had a lasting impression on Jacek Wozniakowski, a graduate student who would become a friend of the pope. The man says that, as a young priest, Father Wojtyla was "a very intelligent man who quickly learned new ways of doing things from what was demanded of him"[18] by the people around him — in the manner of a servant leader.

today because they did not emerge from a vacuum. A large body of research supporting his conclusions has grown up, dating back to the 1950s with the pioneering work of Peter Drucker and supported by the research of Robert Greenleaf, author of the term "servant leader," who published the groundbreaking book *Servant Leadership* in 1977.[19] Support from countless other effective leaders and leadership scholars has built a convincing body of evidence that our traditional image of the dominating, authoritarian leader has nothing to do with truly effective long-term leadership.

History's Best Level 5 Executive

Modern leadership scholars measure leader effectiveness by organizational performance. The key measures of success include how long an organization lasts and how big it grows. If we use those criteria, you can't find a more successful organization than Christianity. While most organizations don't survive their founders, and very few survive a century, Christianity has persisted for almost 2,000 years. In that time, it has grown into the world's largest organization, with 2.1 billion adherents today. If we consider Catholicism alone, it is nearly two millennia old and today includes 1.2 billion members. Clearly, it is an example of unprecedented success. Behind this success must be someone with unprecedented leadership aptitude.

Using Collins' terminology, it's easy to see that Jesus was the model Level 5 executive. He lived and preached humility, and He exercised an unswerving will to fulfill His mission, no matter what the cost. Consider, for example:

- His temptations in the desert when He chose to do His Father's will rather than satisfy His own human hungers.
- His decision to wash His apostles' feet as a way to show them how they should lead others.
- His ordeal in the Garden of Gethsemane, when He submitted to His Father's will despite His own wishes.
- His humiliating suffering and death on the cross as a criminal, while His followers abandoned Him and His persecutors mocked Him.
- His decision to ask the Father to forgive rather than be vengeful to those who were persecuting and killing Him.

Throughout His life, Jesus demonstrated a will that was so focused, it could abandon all self-interest for the sake of His Father's redemptive plan. Many leaders ask their followers to die for them.

Jesus didn't do that. Instead, He chose an absolutely selfless course and died a terrible death for us.

What did it get Him? As He breathed His last breath on the cross, it did not appear that His harvest amounted to much. Let's examine the scene. We see a heartbroken mother, her sister, her friend, and just one disciple consoling one another at the foot of the cross. The soldiers who have crucified Him are casting lots for His clothes. The other disciples have run off to hide. The disciple He has chosen to lead after His ascension into heaven has even denied knowing Him! How could Jesus not be disappointed by this state of affairs?

Despite their betrayal, Jesus did not give up on them. After His resurrection, He sought them out and continued to prepare them for their crucial leadership roles. When He finally delegated the leadership task to them and ascended into heaven, He did not abandon them. Instead, He promised that He would always be with them (Mt 28:20) and sent them the Holy Spirit at Pentecost. As a result, many of the same disciples who had abandoned Him on the cross later mustered the courage and character to die for Him. Peter, who denied knowing Jesus, accepted his own cross years later — and legend has it that he asked that his cross be inverted so that his death would be more humble than his leader's death. Not only has the organization Jesus founded almost 2,000 years ago continued to live and thrive

The Role of Bishops

"Our thoughts today are centered on the bishop's exercise of sacred power. . . . This demands of us a pastoral style inspired by the example of Christ. . . . This apostolic authority is a form of service to the body of Christ. As such, it can only be inspired by and modeled on the self-sacrificing love of the Lord who came among us as a servant and, after stooping to wash the feet of his disciples, commanded them to do as he had done."[20]

POPE JOHN PAUL II

around the world, but some of His followers are still dying for Him. Obviously, Jesus knew something about effective leadership, even by this world's basic standards. As He taught, and as scholars are finally starting to confirm today: Effective leadership for the long term comes from people who see themselves, first and foremost, as servants.

REFLECTION QUESTIONS

- Recall some of the leaders in my own life. Were the most influential ones more like tyrants or servants?
- Am I surprised that the very best leaders share the common trait of humility?
- Can I recall a time when a leader I admired showed great humility? How did it make me feel?
- What is there about Jesus' approach to leadership that encourages me to follow His teaching and example?

"Blessed are the pure in heart, for they will see God."

MATTHEW 5:8

"The issue is the primacy of God. . . . If a man's heart is not good, then nothing else can turn out good either."[21]

POPE BENEDICT XVI

Chapter Five

S¹: Beginning With the Heart

Certainly, effective leadership began on the inside for Jesus. To be a leader, Jesus had to know His values and have His priorities in order. How would He or anyone else know that was the case until He was tested? So, immediately after He was baptized by John the Baptist, a moment that marked the beginning of His public leadership role, He went into the wilderness where He was tested. In St. Matthew's account (Mt 4:1-11), He was first tempted to subdue the natural order to satisfy Himself with material goods. Then He was tempted to subdue the supernatural order by manipulating God's love. Finally, He was tempted to subdue the human order to a personal drive for power and prominence. In every case, He made the selfless choice, the one consistent with His Father's will.

Today, political spinmeisters have developed a whole trade of tricks to make mediocre, venal bureaucrats and demagogues appear to be leaders worthy of our allegiance. Noted author Steven Covey says that in the last century our culture has become more concerned about image than character. Instead of focusing on how to *act like leaders*, we started to focus on how to *look like leaders*.[22] Perhaps that helps to explain why so many duly authorized political and business leaders inspire so little allegiance from us today, and why not a small number of them have earned the ire of stakeholders and regulators alike. When they are called to actually perform like leaders, they fail. And sometimes to cover up their failures, they run afoul of the law. There is, in the end, no substitute for character. To be servant leaders in the image of Jesus, we have to focus on what's inside us. We have to nurture a servant's heart.

But a good heart with its good intentions isn't enough. One of my favorite prayers is, "God, save me from people with *only* good intentions."

To be effective leaders, we need much more than a servant's heart filled with good intentions. We need *heads* with knowledge about what it means to be an S³ Leader in the image of Jesus. We need *hands* to consistently apply what we know, even in times of confusion and crisis. And finally (although from the very start), we need everyday *habits* that fuel our devotion to serve and keep us on track in good times and bad. Unless we take such a holistic approach in our efforts to lead like Jesus, we will find it impossible to make lasting progress.

EGO — Edging God Out

Effective leadership in the image of Jesus begins inside each of us because that's where the biggest impediment to servant leadership is found. Ken Blanchard and Phil Hodges, founders of the Lead Like Jesus movement, call this impediment EGO. Like the psychologist Sigmund Freud's sense of ego, Blanchard and Hodges' EGO has to do with the self. But in Blanchard and Hodges' approach, EGO refers to our human tendency to *Edge God Out*.

As the chart on the next page shows, when we are self-centered, we make our own performance the source of our security and self-worth. We make the self our prime audience and judge. We put ourselves at the center of everything. In effect, we begin to worship the self, making us our own god, while driving out the God who made us and loves us unconditionally.

When life becomes a matter of looking out for the self, we are driven to promote the self and so become prideful. Or we are driven to protect the self and thus become fearful. No matter whether we resort to pride or fear, we are headed down a path that will do us and others great harm. We become alienated from God, other people, our true self, and (because our comparisons distort the truth) finally we become alienated from the reality of God's world. We end up alone and fearful in an imaginary world of our own making.

If we travel the path of fear, we might adopt one of several behaviors. We may hoard information to give ourselves resources others don't have. If we have official power of some sort, we may hide behind our position. We may intimidate others. We may hoard control. We may

EGO SELF-CENTERED: EDGING GOD OUT

Who I worship	My source of security and self-worth	My audience and judge

PRIDE

An overly high opinion of self, exaggerated esteem of self, haughtiness, arrogance.

I say to everyone among you not to think of yourself more highly than you ought to think. (Rom 12:3)

FEAR

An insecure view of the future, which produces self-protection.

Fear of others lays a snare, / but one who trusts in the LORD is secure. (Prov 29:25)

Promoting Self

· Boasting
· Taking all of the credit
· Showing off
· Doing all of the talking
· Demanding all of the attention

Always separates
man from God, other people, himself

Always compares
with others and is never happy

Always distorts
the truth into a false sense of security or fear

Protecting Self

· Hiding behind position
· Withholding information
· Intimidating others
· Hoarding control
· Discouraging honest feedback

© 2005 The Center for Faithwalk Leadership dba Lead Like Jesus. All rights reserved.

react badly to critical but potentially helpful feedback, punishing the messenger to protect the self from the message. We may lie to avoid criticism or to cover our vulnerabilities. We may cheat to get an edge.

The path of pride takes the opposite approach to the same end: protecting the self. It is okay to take some satisfaction in our accomplishments, and that sort of "pride" can be a healthy thing. But in the extreme, pride is an overly high opinion of oneself. We build ourselves up in an effort to convince ourselves and others that we are more important than anyone ought to be. We may brag. We may immerse ourselves in extravagance. We may force our will on others and treat them dismissively. We do these things to convince ourselves that we are more important than other people — and to convince them, too, if we can.

Perhaps pride is just another face of deep-seated fear. Whether or not that's the case, both of these strategies are expressions of the same reality: our own self-centeredness. When we make the self the primary source of security and self-worth, then the purpose of life becomes protecting and exalting the self. The way we do that is by letting ourselves become driven by fear or pride. When our garden is filled with the seeds of fear and pride, three dreaded weeds grow up: comparison, distortion, and ultimately, alienation.

- **Comparison:** If we are focused on promoting and protecting the self, we have to see how we are doing. And the way to see that is to compare our circumstances with the circumstances of others. Do others have more riches, power, or status? If so, we are vulnerable and have to struggle harder to rise above them or protect ourselves from them.

- **Distortion:** If we are focused on our own welfare, we will see reality in terms of what we don't have and others do. From this biased beginning, we are always losing. We can never declare victory, celebrate, and relax until we have all the riches, power, and prestige in the universe. Life becomes a constant battle for more and more.

- **Alienation:** As we carry out this battle, we become more and more alienated from others because we become more inclined to treat them as the enemy. We also become more alienated from God because our involvement in constant conflict forces us to ever more intensely focus on our own welfare at the expense of everyone and everything else, including our self-lessly loving Creator. In fact, as we experience life as an ever larger battle, it becomes ever more difficult to believe that life is animated by love. When we cut ourselves off from God's love, we are also cut off from the truth of our own existence. We reduce life to a war, other people to adversaries in that war, and ourselves to a lonely warrior condemned to fight an ultimately futile battle. Having deprived ourselves of God's love — given to us both directly in life and indirectly through other people — we lose our capacity to love, which is the most precious part of ourselves and the most rewarding part of life. In complete and utter self-centeredness, we may win battle after battle in life, but we ultimately lose the war that we are fighting with life itself.

Of course, our self-centered worlds are fiction. We can sustain the lie that we are our own Master of the Universe only as long as God continues to grant us life. When we die, our self-delusion ends. In contrast, the Creator and the universe He created endure and prevail. This may not seem like a difficult thing to understand, but it certainly is a very difficult thing for human beings to remember. No doubt that's why the Father made it the subject of His very first commandment (Ex 20:2-3; Deut 5:6-7) and why Jesus reiterated it when asked to name the most important commandment: "You shall love the Lord your God with all your heart, and with all your soul, and with all your mind" (Mt 22:37).

REFLECTION QUESTIONS

- Can I think of someone who exercises or has exercised great influence in my life without having a formal position of authority over me? What is or was the basis of his or her power to influence me?
- What are the major values that shape my decisions in life? Would they have to change for me to develop a servant's heart?
- Do I want to change them? Do I think I can?
- What are the major challenges confronting me as I try to develop a servant's heart?
- When have I let pride or fear take over and edge God out of my life?
- What were the long-term results of letting pride or fear rule my life? How would I behave differently today, knowing what I know now?

EGO — Exalting God Only

As humans, we are driven to self-centeredness, which manifests itself as pride or fear, both of which Edge God Out. There is another way to approach life and its leadership challenges which is not futile. Recall Jesus' paradoxical promise, which we hear Him refer to six times in the Gospels: "Those who try to make their life secure will lose it, but those who lose their life will keep it" (Lk 17:33).[23] How do we save our life by losing it? Ken Blanchard and Phil Hodges call this the other kind of EGO — *Exalting God Only*.

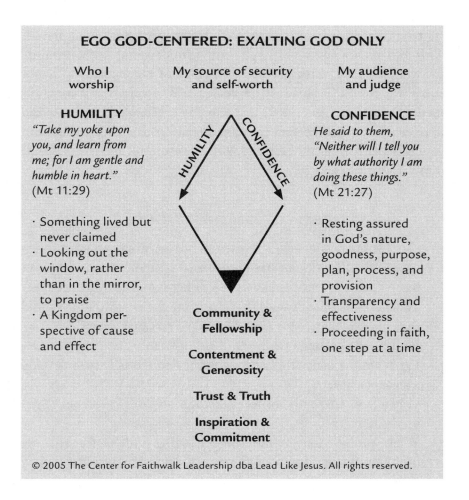

EGO GOD-CENTERED: EXALTING GOD ONLY

Who I worship	My source of security and self-worth	My audience and judge
HUMILITY		**CONFIDENCE**

HUMILITY

"Take my yoke upon you, and learn from me; for I am gentle and humble in heart." (Mt 11:29)

· Something lived but never claimed
· Looking out the window, rather than in the mirror, to praise
· A Kingdom perspective of cause and effect

CONFIDENCE

He said to them, "Neither will I tell you by what authority I am doing these things." (Mt 21:27)

· Resting assured in God's nature, goodness, purpose, plan, process, and provision
· Transparency and effectiveness
· Proceeding in faith, one step at a time

Community & Fellowship

Contentment & Generosity

Trust & Truth

Inspiration & Commitment

© 2005 The Center for Faithwalk Leadership dba Lead Like Jesus. All rights reserved.

When our EGO focuses on *Exalting God Only*, rather than on *Edging God Out*, life is experienced in a very different way, and our leadership role can be lived out in an incredibly effective manner. When God becomes the focus of our worship, the source of our security and self-worth, and our most important audience and judge, then pride and fear have no place in our lives. Instead of clinging to and feeding pride, we abide in humility. Instead of acting out of fear, we move with confidence from one challenge to the next.

The results of our activities are dramatically different, too. We build community and fellowship. We foster contentment and generosity in ourselves and in others. We build trust and increase the flow of trust all around us. We are inspired to increase our capacity and to make greater contributions to the common good. And we inspire others to do the same. Service, contribution, and purpose become the hallmarks of both our individual and collective lives.

The seeming paradox of Jesus' promise becomes clearer. When we live for Jesus' sake — which was, in fact, to exalt God only — we find a new way to live. The heart that beats in us becomes a servant's heart. And the life that heart sustains is the life of a servant leader fashioned in the image of Jesus' own life. Of course, this is never easy. It is always a struggle. And the struggle is lifelong. Fortunately, it's not something we have to endure alone. Jesus knows how difficult it is. Even after having completed His ministry, He knelt in the Garden of Gethsemane and spoke candidly with His Father about His own reluctance to put something ahead of self: "My Father, if it is possible, let this cup pass from me; yet not what I want but what you want" (Mt 26:39). In the end, Jesus was true to His mission. But it wasn't easy for Him, and He knows it won't be easy for you.

Loving God and putting Him first is not an abstract thing. It is concrete, and it involves loving one another as Jesus loves us. The Evangelist says as much: "The commandment we have from him is this: those who love God must love their brothers and sisters also" (1 Jn 4:21). Jesus Himself tells us: "I am the way, and the truth, and the life. No one comes to the Father except through me" (Jn 14:6). All Christians are called to love as Jesus loves — and to lead as Jesus leads.

REFLECTION QUESTIONS

- What is the greatest difficulty I encounter in loving or trying to love God?
- Would I like to love God more? How might I go about it?
- What do I think would be the concrete benefits in my life from *Exalting God Only* rather than *Edging God Out*?

Life's Fundamental Choice: Growing Into the Power to Love

When we are born, we are not able to look after any of our needs. We have natural needs, of course, and we are able to articulate them in a general sense by crying whenever any of them are not met. But as we grow organically, our self-consciousness emerges. At some point, we say that magic word which indicates our self-consciousness has begun. It often happens when someone tries to take something from us. We pull away and declare, "Mine!" At that point, we have become aware that a *me* exists, with needs that have to be met. Now we are a player in the game of looking after ourselves.

Our role will enlarge as we grow. Even if we cannot meet our needs with our own resources, we can identify our needs, prioritize them, and engage others in helping us meet them. Initially, we don't distinguish between needs and wants. *If we want something, we need it, and the whole world is obligated to get it for us.*

Gradually, if we are socialized properly, we will come to recognize, at least in a general way, the difference between needs and wants. We desire a lot of things, but we really need only some of them. We also begin to realize that we share the world with other people who also have desires, some of which are truly essential needs. So gradually we learn that there are boundaries. If we don't consider the wants and needs of others, we are likely to experience resistance trying to satisfy our own wants and needs.

We learn to be considerate for both selfish and unselfish reasons. Yet, we remain most aware of our own needs and wants, so they naturally come first with us. That would be the sum of the human

—————————— IN THE CHURCH ——————————

"Whoever Wants to Be First . . ."

Some Catholics are inclined to think that the vocation of priesthood is more important than the lay vocation. Unfortunately, some of the people who think this way are priests. But the most celebrated priest in the 20th century didn't share this view. Pope John Paul II considered him a hero. Who was he?

Maximilian Kolbe was a Franciscan priest who found himself a prisoner at the German concentration camp of Auschwitz. There he volunteered to give up his life to save a fellow prisoner who was a married man with children.

In June 1979, when Karol Wojtyla returned to his native Poland for the first time as pope, he made it a point to visit Auschwitz. He walked down a path to Block 11, where he went down the steps and found Cell 18, the place where Father Kolbe had given up his life. The pope knelt, prayed, and kissed the floor where Father Kolbe had lain suffering. Next he walked to pray near a wall where firing squads shot prisoners, and on the way he met Franciszek Gajowniczek, then 78, the man Father Kolbe had saved by giving up his own life. Pope John Paul II embraced him.

On October 10, 1982, the pope stood before a quarter of a million people in St. Peter's Square and declared the self-sacrificing priest a saint. John Paul II also declared him a martyr for the faith, even though he had not been directly killed for his beliefs. Yet, St. Maximilian Kolbe had died for a principle of the faith — the God-given dignity of every person — and apparently that was sufficient to make him a martyr in the pope's eyes.

story — and a bloody history it would be — were it not for one other endowment we have: *the power to love.*

Because we have free will, we can choose to value someone or something even more than we value ourselves. Love permits us to decide that the wants and needs of another person are as important to us as our own — or perhaps even more important. Love even permits us to act entirely selflessly, even to offering our lives, our very existence, for the good of another.

At some point in our development, we begin to think about the meaning and purpose of our life. We begin to grapple with some fundamental questions:

- Why am I here?
- What do I want to accomplish?
- Who or what makes my life worth living?
- Who or what can I trust to help me?
- Who or what will I trust with my life?
- Who or what matters most to me?
- For whom or what might I die or kill?
- For whom or what will I live?

As my friend Gregory Pierce puts it, we begin to seek "a mission worthy of our lives."[24] In this process we face the most fundamental choice in human existence: *Will my life be self-centered or other-centered?* If it is centered on someone or something other than myself, who or what will that be? Who or what deserves my life as much as or more than I do?

As Christians we believe that only God, the Giver of all life, is worthy of our ultimate devotion and love, and that when we put God first in our lives, everything else falls into its proper place. Living up to that ideal is a lifelong struggle for most of us. But as Jesus reminds us: "Those who want to save their life will lose it, and those who lose their life for my sake will find it" (Mt 16:25).

―――――――― IN THE FAMILY ――――――――

The Amazing Selflessness of Parents

The one relationship where people are most inclined to be selfless is with their children. Sometimes it even amazes parents just how selfless they can be. If you are a parent, think back to the first time your first little baby came down with a cold. Her lungs were congested, and her breathing was strained. She was so tiny and fragile. No way could you sleep with her struggling for air, even if she stopped crying between gasps and gurgles. So you gently rocked her. Soon you started to talk to God about this amazing little miracle in your embrace. "God, please don't let her be sick like this," you pleaded. Her gasps and gurgles, punctuated with little cries, continued. You started to bargain. "Look, God," you said, "You can take my life if You will spare her from this cold."

You were stunned to hear yourself say it! *My life for her cold? What kind of bargain is that?* In a moment you were sure: "It's a great bargain. I'd give *anything* to see her well again."

Then you wondered: *Where did that come from? Could I be over-reacting? How did I ever become this selfless? When did it happen?* In the same instant you knew the answer: it happened the very moment you first laid eyes on her. For the first time in your life, you had met someone for whom, from the moment you saw her, you would lay down your life. Everything changed for you in that instant.

As the years pass, parents are challenged. There seems to come a point in every child's life where he or she — filled with passion, speaking now with the whole heart, mind, and soul — turns to each parent and screams, "I hate you!" In that moment, a parent faces a question and a choice: Am I in this relationship to give love or to get it?

If the parent's primary purpose is to *give* love, the child's behavior is hurtful but not a crisis. Parental love does not depend on the child because it is *unconditional*.

However, if for some reason the parent relies on the parent-child relationship to *get* love, the moment is filled with crisis. If, from the parent's perspective, the child's primary role is to give the parent love, the child's words and actions will be devastating. The parent is faced with the task of defending himself or herself, and so faces the choice of striking back in prideful anger or of withdrawing emotionally in fear, hoping to minimize the awful pain. In either case, the child loses by not getting the love that a child needs from a parent in order to grow into a healthy adult.

The "good news" of the Gospel (*gospel* means "good news") is that God loves us even more than He loves Himself. Not only that, He loves us even more than He loves His own child — which every loving parent knows is much more than one can ever love oneself. Love — which opens us up to the possibility of a truly large life purpose — is the source of life. It is the creative force by which God brings us into existence. "God is love" (1 Jn 4:8). Love is what moves Him, and it is how He expresses Himself. The universe exists — as well as each molecule and atom and subatomic particle, each and every grain of sand, and each and every person in each and every minute of life — as nothing but the material expression of God's infinite and selfless love for us.

REFLECTION QUESTIONS

- What are my greatest needs in life?
- What are some things that I want but I know I don't really need?
- Have I ever risked neglecting my greatest needs in order to get something I wanted?
- Are there things in my life worth dying for? And are they the same things that I live for? If not, why not?
- Can I think of a time in my life when I should have been giving love but instead focused on getting love? How do I feel about that now?
- Can I think of a time in my life when I really was a love giver? How do I feel about that now?

"When anyone hears the word of the kingdom and does not understand it, the evil one comes and snatches away what is sown in the heart."

<small>MATTHEW 13:19</small>

"I don't believe leadership can be taught, but it can be learned."[25]

<small>WARREN BENNIS</small>

Chapter Six

S¹: Developing a Servant's Head

We cannot practice true servant leadership unless we have a servant's heart. A servant's heart is the seed we need to grow into a true servant leader in the image of Jesus. But as Jesus' parable of the sower and the seed makes clear, a seed cannot grow on its own. It needs to be planted in good soil. The seed that is a servant's heart needs the soil of a servant's head, hands, and habits. Without this soil, our servant's heart is like the seed in Jesus' parable that fell on rocky ground: "When they hear the word, they immediately receive it with joy. But they have no root, and endure only for a while; then, when trouble or persecution arises on account of the word, immediately they fall away" (Mk 4:16-17).

The commitment to be a servant leader, which is a matter of the heart, is inevitably followed by real-life challenges to be a servant leader. If our commitment is not rooted in knowledge about what it means to be a servant leader and exactly how we can accomplish this goal, our commitment will soon wane and die. It is not enough to want to be a servant leader. We also have to learn *what it means* to be a servant (head) and *how we can practice* servant leadership on a day-to-day, relationship-to-relationship basis (hands). Finally, we have to learn *how to sink the roots of servanthood deep* into the soil of our character (habits) so that our commitment holds up in the face of life's inevitable challenges. We focus now on how we develop the head of a servant leader. There is no better place to start than with the teaching of the perfect servant leader, Jesus Christ Himself.

Two Dimensions of Leadership

In the development of His apostles' leadership capacity, Jesus recognized that leadership has two dimensions: *vision* and *application* (implementation). The vision part of leadership involves articulating the purpose of a group, whether it is a family or a multinational organization. Leaders address why the group exists and what it does. In this dimension, leaders exercise authority by making decisions about what the group will and will not do, as well as how its tasks will get done and what resources will be targeted to achieve the group's ends. Leaders may choose to involve other people in developing a vision, and often that is a wise course. But they cannot delegate this dimension of leadership to others. Ultimately, leaders are accountable *to* and *for* the vision of the group they are leading.

If vision was the only thing effective leadership involved, it would look very much like our traditional view of leadership (see the diagram below). Leaders would decide what the group does and direct how it is done. Followers would do what they are told to do in the manner in which they are told to do it. In such a model, it is not difficult to see how those in leadership — reserving for themselves all the power to make decisions — might "lord it over" everyone in the group. This model can't be criticized for its simplicity. But there is a serious problem with it. It is simplistic. It considers only one of the two dimensions of effective leadership. And since the dimension it ignores seems to be the more important one, this model is not particularly helpful in achieving excellence.[26]

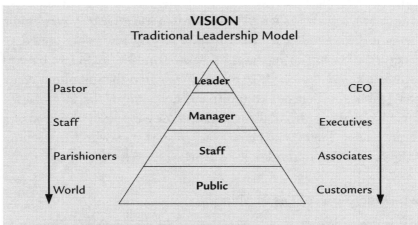

VISION
Traditional Leadership Model

Pastor	Leader	CEO
Staff	Manager	Executives
Parishioners	Staff	Associates
World	Public	Customers

© 2005 The Center for Faithwalk Leadership dba Lead Like Jesus. All rights reserved.

What's missing from this traditional model of leadership is the other aspect of leadership: *implementation*. Once a group's purpose is clear, it has to apply its resources — including especially its human resources — to achieve its purpose. To do that effectively, the organizational pyramid must be inverted so that the leaders are at the bottom of the pyramid, where they can focus on helping their so-called subordinates succeed. Turning the pyramid upside down to achieve the group's vision may sound strange, but parents do it all the time, generally without even thinking about it. In doing so, they achieve incredible developmental success.

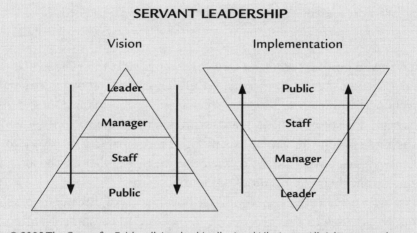

SERVANT LEADERSHIP

Vision   Implementation

Leader   Public
Manager   Staff
Staff   Manager
Public   Leader

© 2005 The Center for Faithwalk Leadership dba Lead Like Jesus. All rights reserved.

It's in the *implementation*, or execution, part of servant leadership where the role of *servant* comes to the fore. Effective leaders know their purpose is not to catch their subordinates doing wrong, but rather to help them succeed. Imagine the top manager who goes to his annual review and tells his CEO: "We didn't make any of our goals this year. But I think I've done a great job as a leader because I can tell you where every one of my team members screwed up. In fact, I've got it all quantified right here in this big report. I'm hoping you think it's the kind of quality work that is deserving of a big raise."

If a person's job is to *audit* the performance of others, such a report might be worthy of a raise. But if a person's job is to lead a group effort

A Pope Drops the Symbol of the Crown

At Pope John Paul II's investiture ceremony, he decided that he would not be crowned with the papal tiara, called a *triregnum*, because it had come to be seen as a symbol of the pope's temporal power, and he said the Church is not a church of power but a church of evangelical witness.

According to biographer George Weigel, the pope wanted to be perfectly clear about the meaning of the papacy and, indeed, the whole Church: "service, service with a single purpose — to ensure that all the People of God share in the threefold mission of Christ and always remain under the power of the Lord."[27]

to *produce* a product, *provide* a service, or *close* a sale, then fixing blame is not getting the job done. Even CEOs who work and live in palatial splendor, being paid millions of dollars per year, won't last long if all they can do is provide their boards with detailed explanations for why everyone else on the payroll is sinking the company. Effective leaders always foster the success of their followers, whether on the job, at home, or in their communities or churches.

Performance is the key, no matter how boards of directors, bosses, and, yes, donors to charities decide to measure it. Presumably, all the people in the organization are there because they have a contributing role to play in the organization's performance. (If not, simply removing them from the payroll will improve performance.) Since everyone in the organization presumably has a contributing role to play, individual performance is critical to organizational performance. That means, at each level of the organization, a leader is obliged to assure that his or her followers are making the contributions they were hired to make. In a word, the leader's task is to make sure all of his or her people *succeed*.

A Short History of Human Management

Over the centuries, bosses have employed a host of ways to assure their people's success. From the dawn of humanity until the early

1900s, the focus was on *compliance*. A good model of a leader focused on compliance is the galley ship owner who strapped his slaves to oars, hired some big thugs to motivate the slackers with whips, and added a drummer to the payroll to keep everybody in rhythm. There are two problems with compliance systems. First, they are expensive; and second, they never get more than minimum performance out of people. On the galley ship, no slave ever woke up in the morning and declared, "It's a great day! Let's do our very best and see if we can go faster than we've ever done before." Instead, in a compliance model, people need constant prodding to do anything at all. That means the thugs with whips must be ever vigilant. Since spans of control are short, several thugs must be employed. While the thugs and drummer don't contribute anything directly to output, they still must be

---

IN THE CHURCH

Pope John Paul II's First Public Prayer: "Make Me a Servant"

In Pope John Paul II's first public prayer before the vast audience at his investiture ceremony in Rome, and the millions more watching on television around the world, he asked: "Christ, make me become and remain the servant of your unique power, the servant of your sweet power, the servant of your power that knows no eventide. Make me a servant. Indeed, the servant of your servants."

He turned to speak to his audience and said: "Be not afraid to welcome Christ and accept his power. Help the Pope and all those who wish to serve Christ and with Christ's power to serve the human person and the whole of mankind." Then he greeted people in several languages and asked a favor of the people: "Pray for me. Help me to be able to serve you. Amen."

Finally he walked toward the huge crowd in St. Peter's Square. George Weigel reports that as John Paul II greeted and blessed a group of handicapped people in wheelchairs, a small boy broke through the restraints to hand the pope a bouquet of flowers. A cleric tried to "shoo" him away. The pope interceded, grabbed the boy, and hugged him.[28]

━━━━━━━━━━━━━━IN THE CHURCH━━━━━━━━━━━━━━

The Pope's Titles Change Over the Years

Three changes in the pope's titles made in the Vatican's official yearbook, the *Annuario Pontificio*, over the past 40 years show a growing recognition of the importance of servant leadership in the highest ranks of the Church.

In the 1969 edition, Pope Paul VI made two changes. He dropped the phrase "gloriously reigning" and added the title "servant of the servants of God."

In the 2006 edition, Pope Benedict XVI dropped the title "patriarch of the West."

Cardinal Achille Silvestrini, retired prefect of the Congregation for Eastern Churches, said the deletion was a "sign of ecumenical sensitivity" on the part of the pope.[29]

fed, so a lot of resources get spent achieving no better than minimum performance.

In the early-20th century, some people noticed the high cost of compliance. Arguing that "you can catch more flies with honey than with vinegar," they said that organizations would be more productive if they fostered *cooperation*. If people wanted to do what they were hired to do and were taught how to do it on their own, fewer overseers would be needed and operations could be more efficient. By and large *cooperation* turned out to offer some distinct advantages over *compliance*. However, it did not represent a change in the leadership task. That task was still simply to get followers to do what the leaders wanted them to do in the way that the leaders wanted them to do it.

Near the latter half of the 20th century, as the Information Age came to full blossom, more work became "knowledge work," and it grew harder to measure productivity, especially on a short-term basis. But some organizations performed appreciably better than others. Studies showed that these high-performing organizations had systems that fostered *contribution* on the part of everyone. In such systems, the leadership task changes. Leaders are charged with getting everything possible out of followers — including their ideas and innovations.

Allen Randolph and Ken Blanchard call this "empowerment," adding that it means "letting people bring their brains to work."[30] In these contexts, servant leaders really shine. Today, it's generally recognized that the best-performing organizations are those that are able to harness their people's drive to contribute to their organizations' success. We'll explore that aspect of servant leadership in the next chapter, which describes how to develop a servant's *hands*.

---IN THE FAMILY---

How Leadership's Two Dimensions Work for Parents and Children

Let's see how effective parents routinely "turn the pyramid upside down" in a nurturing family. The parents are the family's leaders. Their children come to them completely dependent and helpless. Initially, the parents must take care of their every need. At the same time, the parents develop visions for their family and for their children. ("My daughter the lawyer" or "my son the NFL quarterback." We parents can set the bar high.) Children quickly begin to blossom: to walk, talk, and look after some basic needs. They may or may not show any promise for a career in medicine, law, or sports superstardom. But as children develop new interests and attitudes, parents often change their visions for them. ("My daughter the starving artist" or "my son the professional gamer.")

After a few years, the child faces the critical challenge of school. The parents help the child get off to a good start in many ways. Their "training program" really began years ago, but now the focus is clear. Parents buy the child clothes and supplies needed for school. They register her at a school. On the first day, they help her find the door to her classroom and go with her to meet her teacher. After that, on a daily basis, they continue to see that she wakes up on time, eats breakfast, gets all her needed papers and supplies together, and gets in the car or heads to the bus stop in a timely fashion. Their focus is on helping the child succeed.

Parents will also monitor their child's performance. But their purpose is not to catch her doing wrong and punish her. Instead, their purpose is to help contribute to her development and improvement. If the parent gets a report that the child is misbehaving, some punishment may be in order. However, if the parents get a report that their child is having difficulty in a particular class, they don't immediately punish her for that. Instead, they might ask the teacher if their child is applying herself or goofing off. Once it's determined that the child is trying but struggling, the parents will devote extra time to helping the child learn the material. Usually, this extra time and attention pays great dividends. The child succeeds at learning the material and moves on to the next challenge.

Eventually, if all goes well, the child becomes an adolescent and begins to wonder how a genius like her could have such idiotic parents. This is a time when parents pray for patience: more growth is likely — although not soon.

Children develop so dramatically from birth to adolescence not just because nature is on the side of development. Effective families are incredibly nurturing places. What makes them so successful is that their leaders (parents) are true servant leaders who put the developmental needs of their children ahead of their own well-being. The system works so well that we take it for granted. But step back and look at the results! The nurturing practices of effective families, although commonplace, are truly revolutionary. In healthy families, we see tiny, completely helpless and dependent infants develop into literate, competent, and caring young adults, able to continue learning and growing on their own.

Imagine if our workplaces nurtured growth and development in the same way. What parents accomplish as amateur leaders (trust me: all of us parents are amateurs) is incredible when compared to what is accomplished in workplaces by credentialed professionals. Biology aside, the problem is that too many "professional" leaders don't have a commitment to nurture people, and to help them grow and increase their capacity to perform. Leaders are too busy "looking out for Number One."

Ironically, it's only when we take our commitment seriously, as servant leaders, to nurture others, that we really start "looking out for Number One," because that's when we see the same sort of dramatic performance improvements in our workplaces, communities, clubs, and friendship circles as we see in most homes.

REFLECTION QUESTIONS

- What are my visions for the relationships I care most about (marriage, family, company, team, parish, charity, community organization)?
- How can I serve others in these relationships to help bring my visions to fruition?
- In my key relationships, do I focus on other persons' compliance, cooperation, or contributions?
- Do I think that I might better foster my vision by changing my focus? How might I begin to do that?

Let the favor of the Lord our God be upon us,
and prosper for us the work of our hands —
O prosper the work of our hands!

PSALM 90:17

On the sabbath he began to teach in the synagogue, and many who heard him were astounded. They said, "Where did this man get all this? What is this wisdom that has been given to him? What deeds of power are being done by his hands!"

MARK 6:2

"The leaders who work most effectively, it seems to me, never say 'I.' And that's not because they have trained themselves not to say 'I.' They don't think 'I.' They think 'we'; they think 'team.' They understand their job to be to make the team function. They accept the responsibility and don't sidestep it, but 'we' get the credit. This is what creates trust, what enables you to get the task done." [31]

PETER DRUCKER

Chapter Seven

S¹: Extending a Servant's Hands

To lead like Jesus, it's important that we care about more than ourselves (a servant's heart), and it's important that we understand what's required of us as a leader (a servant's head). But we also need to know *how* to put our concern and knowledge to practical use on a day-to-day basis (a servant's *hands*). Let's consider now the four skills that are required to have a servant's hands.

- Intimacy
- Diagnosis
- Flexibility
- Partnering for Performance

1. Intimacy

The effective leader recognizes that each person is unique. If we want to contribute to every person's development, we have to understand as intimately as possible where they are on the developmental continuum and how we can best help them continue to grow. The importance of this kind of intimacy is especially apparent in the nurturing family. Parents often tell you that they felt relaxed when they anticipated the birth of their second child because they had already been through the process once and believe they had developed some expertise. Then they confess: "Boy, was I wrong about that! When the second one came along, I learned I had to take everything I assumed I knew from having the first child, throw it out the window, and start learning all over again."

That's true in the workplace and in our communities and churches as well. While people go through common developmental stages, no two of us have quite the same mix of gifts or develop exactly along the same lines. Servant leaders recognize the individual, God-given dignity of each person and seek to optimize the development of each person individually. To do that, servant leaders must exercise humility by continually observing and listening to each person for whom they are responsible rather than assuming that they know everything that needs to be known to assist that person's development. If we want to be effective leaders, we have to recognize the uniqueness of every person we encounter.

2. Diagnosis

Once we recognize that people are unique, we can begin to address their unique needs. Fortunately, when it comes to accomplishing any task or fulfilling any responsibility, these needs tend to exist along a common developmental framework. Because Jesus would have been trained as a carpenter by his foster father, Joseph, Ken Blanchard and Phil Hodges use the language of the trades to describe the stages in this developmental framework.[32] At first, people are *novices*. As they grow in knowledge, they become *apprentices*. As they continue to grow, they become *journeymen*. If growth continues after that, they eventually become *masters*, who are able to teach others how to move along the developmental framework. Servant leaders know where each of their followers is with respect to each of the tasks they are expected to perform.

3. Flexibility

At each stage of development, a person's needs are different:

- *A novice* needs a lot of direction. Since he knows so little, if he is given too much discretion, a lot could go wrong. He could be a danger to himself and others. His behavior has to be monitored closely. He needs a leader who can give him *direction*. But as he learns the basics, he becomes an apprentice and his leadership needs change.

- *An apprentice* knows how to do the basic work that his job entails, so he doesn't need to be directed in every step of every task, and he doesn't have to be monitored constantly. However, at this stage the initial excitement he felt in landing a new job and learning new skills may begin to wear off, and he may need some affirmation and encouragement. He needs a leader who can be a *coach*, someone who can help keep him motivated as the lessons he needs to learn become more difficult and complex. If the apprentice continues to grow, eventually he will become a journeyman.

- *A journeyman* knows how to do all the work he needs to do and how it has to be coordinated with other work processes. Thus, he is able to make some sound decisions about how he organizes and does his work. It would be a waste of expensive resources for a leader to stand over him, watching his work constantly, and the worker would probably come to resent that, making him even less productive. Now he needs a leader who can *support* him, encouraging him to make sound decisions and praising him for his better-than-average performance. If that happens, he may come to master his job.

- *A master/teacher* knows his job so well that he may be the organization's expert about it. In all likelihood, he knows more about his job's particular details than any of his supervisors. Not only is he a master at his job, achieving excellent performance, but he may also very well be the best person to teach others about the work that he does. Now he needs a leader who can *delegate* the job and its responsibilities to him, and encourage him to share his knowledge with others who still have more to learn.

Jesus demonstrated just this sort of leadership flexibility with His own apostles. As soon as He chose them, He gave them all sorts of detailed instructions. In Matthew 10:5-15, we hear Him tell them precisely where to go and not go, what to pack, what to say, what to do, how to find helpers, how to locate a place to stay, and how to react to hosts and hostesses. His leadership with these novices is completely *directive*.

Later, after the apostles have been following His directions for a while and can be considered apprentices, we see in Matthew 17:14-20 how Jesus' leadership style changes to serve their changing needs. A man comes to Jesus to report that His disciples have been unable to cure his son. Jesus cures the young man. That prompts His apostles to ask Him later in private why they couldn't get the job done. Like a *coach*, He tells them what the problem is with their performance. But He also gives them hope and encourages them, telling them that if they can muster just a bit of faith "nothing will be impossible for you" (Mt 17:21).

Recognizing that each apostle would have developed in a unique way at his own pace, we find Peter in the role of journeyman relatively early in the Gospel of Matthew (14:22-33). Here we read that the apostles are in a boat in the middle of the night. The boat is miles from shore, struggling against the wind and being tossed by waves. Suddenly, the apostles see Jesus walking on the water toward their boat. They think it is a ghost, and they're filled with fear. Jesus reassures them. Then Peter, leader of the crew, is apparently ready to make his own mark. He asks Jesus to command him to walk on the water, too. Jesus supports Peter's request and invites him to get out of the boat. Peter gets out of the boat and begins to walk toward Jesus. But soon his fears get the best of him and he begins to sink. "Lord, save me!" he shouts. Jesus responds immediately, extending His hand and pulling him to safety while asking Peter why he had doubted. Here we see Jesus in a *supporting* role, encouraging Peter to extend himself, helping him recover when it turns out he has overextended himself, and reminding him of where he has to improve in order to continue developing in his role.

At the Last Supper, we see Jesus in a similar supporting role. He must address Judas' betrayal, Peter's denial, and the fact that He will soon be turning over His work to the apostles. Although He knows they are not quite ready for that, He expresses His own humility and His great confidence in them when He tells them that "the one who believes in me will also do the works that I do and, in fact, will do greater works than these" (Jn 14:12). As we know, His confidence in them will not be immediately rewarded. Soon they will abandon Him and hide. But effective leadership requires great persistence and patience, and Jesus provides us with a superb model of these virtues.

After Jesus' suffering, death, and resurrection, we read that the apostles are still driven by fear. They have gathered in a room and locked the door "for fear of the Jews" (Jn 20:19). Suddenly, Jesus is there among them. Today we might assume that the sight of Jesus would have calmed their fears. But maybe that wasn't the case at all. Maybe after having abandoned Jesus in His darkest hour, the apostles were terrified to have Him suddenly appear before them. What would they have heard, for example, if they were disciples of New York real estate mogul Donald Trump, star of the television show *The Apprentice*? Chances are, the words "You're fired!" would have sounded in their ears. What does Jesus say? "Peace be with you" (Jn 20:19).

Later, the apostle Thomas, who was not present in the Upper Room, expresses doubt that Jesus appeared to the others, what does Jesus do? Instead of taking offense, He appears to the group again a week later and invites the skeptical Thomas to touch His wounds and verify for himself that the Lord is really there with them. It's clear that Jesus focuses on the apostles' development after His resurrection, for elsewhere in the Gospel we read that He continued teaching them and that "he opened their minds to understand the scriptures" (Lk 24:45).

Finally, just before His ascension into heaven, Jesus addresses the apostles as a group of masters/teachers. He tells them:

> "All authority in heaven and on earth has been given to me. Go therefore and make disciples of all nations, baptizing them in the name of the Father and of the Son and of the Holy Spirit, and teaching them to obey everything that I have commanded you. And remember, I am with you always, to the end of the age." (Mt 28:18-20)

Here we see Jesus in a *delegating* role. He is turning over His work to others, but not abandoning them.

4. Partnering for Performance

Whether we find ourselves at work, at home, or serving in our community or church, generally we have more than one job to do. At work, especially, people generally have a multitude of tasks to accomplish, and frequently new ones are added even if old ones do not go away. One of the greatest mistakes leaders make is assuming that each follower is at a single stage of development regarding all the things he or she must do. In fact, the same person can be a novice in one area and a master/teacher in another at the same time. When working with children, we are always teaching them new things, so we tend to be more aware of the fact that they may be master readers and yet novice mathematicians. With adults, we are more inclined to forget that when they are given a new task or a new position, they are novices in regard to it even if they are masters at other things. It's true that many endowments, emotional and technical, transfer from one task to another. But not all skills transfer all the time. Even veterans in a profession find themselves as novices facing new tasks from time to time.

That's why the most effective leader-follower relationships occur when both the leader and the follower agree on the follower's level of development regarding each task, and the style of leadership needed for the follower to be most effective at that particular task. We call this *partnering for performance*, and it provides the best environment in which a follower can consistently achieve high performance across a wide variety of tasks, duties, and competencies.[33] In a good partnering-for-performance relationship, leader and follower meet often to update their consensus regarding the follower's developmental level and needs in each of his or her areas of responsibility. The goal of both leader and follower is to help the follower reach the success that the organization is relying on him or her to achieve for the good of all.

Fixed on Mission

An effective servant leader will work faithfully to diagnose the developmental needs of his or her followers, will be flexible in trying to meet those needs in an optimal way, and will humbly engage in a partnership with followers in seeking the best ways to enhance their performance and development. But there is one area in which a servant leader cannot be flexible, and again Jesus modeled this reality.

When it came to His mission, Jesus was not flexible. He was absolutely and consistently committed to do the will of His Father, and He never wavered from that commitment — not even at the cost of His life. He acknowledged in the Garden of Gethsemane that His suffering and death were not what He desired for Himself. Yet He subordinated His human drive to save Himself and, instead, submitted to an agonizing and humiliating death in order to do the will of His Father.

At the same time, Jesus recognized that part of His mission was to develop people to carry on His work. To achieve that end, He showed incredible flexibility in meeting the developmental needs of His followers. Eventually, His commitment to the development of His apostles was rewarded. The same men who had doubted, disappointed, and disappeared when He was arrested ended up turning over their lives to His mission. Most of them were so committed that they even gave up their lives for that mission. Jesus clearly showed us what it means to have the *hands of a servant*, and how true servant leadership can unleash incredible commitment, development, and performance on the part of other people.

REFLECTION QUESTIONS

- I will consider the key relationships with others in my life, including in my work, and the key processes in which I interact with these other people. In each of the key processes I have identified, at what stage of development is each of the persons with whom I interact?
- How might I serve each of them better in his or her current stage of development?
- How might I serve each of them so that he or she continues to develop and move into more advanced developmental stages?
- How would my life be better if each of them advanced to the next stage during the next year?

"Truly, matters in the world are in a bad state; but if you and I begin in earnest to reform ourselves, a really good beginning will have been made."

ST. PETER OF ALCANTARA

"In all created things discern the providence and wisdom of God, and in all things give Him thanks."

ST. TERESA OF ÁVILA

"If we want to lead like Jesus, we have to become like Jesus."[34]

KEN BLANCHARD AND PHIL HODGES

Chapter Eight

S¹: Cultivating a Servant's Habits

If we want to be servant leaders, we have no better model than Jesus Christ. Of course, many people have different, even conflicting images or models of Jesus in their own minds. Some see Him primarily as a great institution builder. Others see Him as a great revolutionary. But there is one thing theologians of every Christian tradition agree on: *Jesus' life was absolutely God-centered.* He was completely and consistently focused on doing the will of His Father, and this was more important to Him than life itself. As such, He was a completely selfless leader. Perhaps we can never be as focused and selfless as Jesus was. But we can continually move closer to the ideal He gave us. To do that, we must refocus, recalibrate, and recommit ourselves on a daily basis. Here are nine habits that will help Catholics do this:

- Practice solitude.
- Pray daily.
- Read Scripture.
- Worship and receive the sacraments regularly.
- Explore the lives and reflections of saints and Christian scholars.
- Consider sacramentals and devotions that flourish in the Church.
- Accept and model unconditional love.
- Serve others.
- Build community.

1. Practice Solitude

When we experience failure or frustration, we can become discouraged and lose heart. When we experience success, we can puff ourselves up with pride. In either case, we do damage to our servant's heart and lose our focus on our mission in this life. In solitude, God can help us find some perspective on both our failures and successes, and help us refocus on our purpose as a child of God whom He calls to be a leader in this world.

No matter how rushed or hectic our life is, it's important that we find time to be alone with God, even if it's only for a few minutes a day. Perhaps it's before other family members rise in the morning. Maybe it's in the shower. Maybe it's in the car on the way to or from work, or both. Perhaps it's just a few minutes at our desk or at the kitchen table when our child is napping. Perhaps it's for a brief period in bed just before we fall asleep. Solitude is not always easy to find, but we need it for our spiritual, mental, and physical health.

It's helpful to remind ourselves that Jesus made time for solitude at every important juncture in His life: before He began His public ministry (Mt 4:1-11); before He chose His apostles (Lk 6:12-13); when He heard of the death of St. John the Baptist (Mt 14:13); after He fed 5,000 with fish and bread (Mt 14:23); and as His suffering and death approached (Mt 21:17).

2. Pray Daily

Sometimes we seem to regard prayer like we do reading directions: "When all else fails, read the directions . . . and when that fails, pray." But if we want to lead like Jesus, we should make prayer our *first resort*, not our last, conscious that we are always in God's presence.

As hectic and disheartening as Jesus' life became from time to time, He always took time for prayer. It's no surprise that in three of the five instances cited above where Jesus sought solitude, it's also explicitly mentioned that He prayed. On the last night of His life, He prayed extensively — at table with His disciples, where He summarizes the point of His life and ministries (Jn 17), and then in the Garden of Gethsemane (Mt 26:36-44; Mk 14:32-39; and Lk 22:39-44), until the soldiers arrested Him.

It is good to begin and end our days with prayer, and it is good to pray regularly throughout the day, even if our prayer is just a moment's mindfulness that God is always with us. Some couples find it helpful to end their day by praying together, often in each other's embrace.

On a more formal level, the Catholic Church gives us a great opportunity for daily communal prayer by providing us with daily Mass in most churches. We are not expected to participate in daily Mass, but it is there for us *if we want it*. On that basis, countless millions find it a helpful, hope-filled way to spend a half hour of their day. (Visit our website, *www.YeshuaLeader.com*, to learn more about spontaneous prayer, prayer as talking to God, the ACTS method of prayer, and other tips for improving your prayer life.)

3. Read Scripture

Reading Scripture on a daily basis is a fine way to recalibrate ourselves as servants of God striving to lead like Jesus. We can develop our own system for choosing what and how much to read, or if we prefer, there are many guides and commentaries to help us. Mass, of course, offers brief scriptural passages for our reflection. Even if we don't attend daily Mass, we can get a list of those daily readings in books and on the Web. Many of these sources offer brief commentaries or reflections to help us connect Scripture's insights to our own everyday lives. There is no greater source of God's revelation to the world than holy Scripture, so it behooves us to read, study, and reflect on it regularly — daily, if we can possibly manage it. (For a list of links and guides to help us appreciate and understand Scripture and use it for our daily enrichment, visit our website: *www.YeshuaLeader.com*.)

4. Worship and Receive the Sacraments Regularly

The person who seeks to lead like Jesus will see worship and the sacraments as opportunities provided by the Church to assist us in becoming more like Jesus with each passing day. Chief among the sacraments is the Eucharist, which Vatican II called the "source and summit of the Christian life."[35]

We Catholics believe in the Real Presence of Jesus in the Sacrament of the Eucharist. That means that when we receive the Eucharist, we are inviting and receiving Jesus (His Body, Blood, Soul, and Divinity) into our very being. Frequent reception of the Eucharist is an important way to get and stay on track in our quest to be a servant leader. The Sacraments of Baptism and Confirmation can only be received once in life; and the Sacrament of Matrimony is only received once, unless a person remarries after the death of his or her spouse. The Sacrament of the Anointing of the Sick is received only rarely. Few Catholics know that at one time the Sacrament of Penance and Reconciliation could be received just once in a person's life, but later its reception was liberalized, and today frequent reconciliation is encouraged. No matter how often we avail ourselves of the sacraments, it's good to remember that the Church faithfully offers them to assist us in leading the kind of life Jesus calls us to lead.

Understanding and Benefiting From Scripture

The Bible is not like other books. It is a collection of many books, and it is the inspired word of God. The Second Vatican Council explains:

> Since, therefore, all that the inspired authors, or sacred writers, affirm should be regarded as affirmed by the Holy Spirit, we must acknowledge that the books of Scripture, firmly, faithfully and without error, teach that truth which God, for the sake of our salvation, wished to see confided to the sacred Scriptures. Thus, "all Scripture is inspired by God, and profitable for teaching, for reproof, for correction and for training in righteousness, so that the man of God may be complete, equipped for every good work" (2 Tim 3:16-17).[36]

But being truthful does not mean that we believe the Scriptures are literally factual in every instance. As the council fathers explained:

> Seeing that, in sacred Scripture, God speaks through men in human fashion, it follows that the interpreter of sacred

Scriptures, if he is to ascertain what God has wished to communicate to us, should carefully search out the meaning which the sacred writers really had in mind, that meaning which God had thought well to manifest through the medium of their words.

In determining the intention of the sacred writers, attention must be paid, *inter alia*, to "literary forms for the fact is that truth is differently presented and expressed in the various types of historical writing, in prophetical and poetical texts," and in other forms of literary expression. Hence the exegete must look for that meaning which the sacred writer, in a determined situation and given the circumstances of his time and culture, intended to express and did in fact express, through the medium of a contemporary literary form.[37]

Perhaps you are wondering: How can truth be expressed in a nonfactual way? My grandmother used to say of a downpour, "It's raining cats and dogs." No animals fell from the sky, but she expressed the truth in a figurative way. When we insist that Scripture be read only as a historical record, this may blind us to some profound truths expressed in other ways by its authors.

There's great benefit to reading Scripture no matter how we do it. You'll find inspiration and guidance everywhere. The New Testament is much easier to understand than the Old Testament. However, Old Testament books like Psalms, Proverbs, and Sirach (also known as Ecclesiasticus) are easy to read and contain great insights and everyday wisdom.

5. Explore the Lives and Reflections of Saints and Christian Scholars

Our Catholic tradition includes the identification of many saints — people especially honored because their lives serve as exemplary models to help us live as faithful servants of God. Many of them left writings that can help lead us to a closer relationship with the Lord. Helping people develop closer relationships with God is, in fact, the whole point of identifying saints. We don't worship saints. At most, we venerate

An Example From the Master

Immediately he made his disciples get into the boat and go on ahead to the other side, to Bethsaida, while he dismissed the crowd. After saying farewell to them, he went up on the mountain to pray.

MARK 6:45-46

them, which means to look on them with feelings of deep respect. If we pray to saints, it is not in the same way that we pray to God. When we pray to saints, it is always to ask them to intercede for us with God, just as we might ask our relatives who have died to pray for us to God. (In fact, it's likely that some or all of your relatives are saints in their own right. A person does not have to be canonized to be a saint — and as Catholics, we formally celebrate that fact on November 1, All Saints' Day.)

Some people find it helpful to reflect on the life or writings of a *patron saint* — someone who shares their name, their profession, or some other life connection. Some saints' lives were so remarkable that they attract the devotion of many Catholics. Chief among these, of course, is Mary, the Virgin Mother of God, who was Jesus' first disciple, and who selflessly carried Him, nurtured Him, and suffered His terrible loss for the sake of God's plan of salvation. Other saints who enjoy special prominence among the faithful include St. Joseph, St. Francis of Assisi, St. Patrick, St. Anthony, and St. Thérèse of Lisieux (also known as the "Little Flower"), to name just a few.

Hundreds of works by or about various saints are available in print and on audio and video media. Some of their writings are long; others are brief. Some are intellectual; others are practical. Some are of a broad spiritual nature; others are focused on one aspect of our faith life. Of course, not everything ever written is for every interest or taste. There is so much to choose from that you can afford to be picky — in fact, you'll have to make choices. A wonderfully rich and diverse body of thought exists as a great treasure of our Church's tradition, to help you develop a servant's habits in your own life. Our general advice is two-fold:

- *Follow your heart* by exploring writers, topics, or historical times that are most interesting to you.
- *Stretch yourself* a little bit so that you continue to grow in your faith.

6. Consider Sacramentals and Devotions That Flourish in the Church

In trying to center our lives on God, and to lead like Jesus in all the roles we are called to fill, we find that the Church offers us many forms of devotional assistance. There are, for example, the sacramentals — *objects* and *rituals* to help us be more mindful of God's loving presence in our lives.

- *Sacramental objects* include crucifixes, rosaries, icons of Jesus and the saints, incense, candles, ashes, palms, holy oils, holy water, and holy vessels such as a chalice and a monstrance.
- *Sacramental rituals* include the many ways to pray the Rosary; the Sign of the Cross; the Stations of the Cross; bowing before reception of the Eucharist and other times to show respect for God; genuflecting before entering a church pew or kneeling at certain times during the liturgy; various blessings; and the washing of feet during the Holy Thursday liturgy.

Respond to those that appeal to you; don't be troubled by those that don't. If you would like to light a candle to help you focus in solitude and prayer, go ahead — but you are under no compulsion to light a candle. If contemplating one favorite set of mysteries makes praying the Rosary more appealing to you, by all means indulge your passion. But you are not required to recite the Rosary. If participating in the Stations of the Cross with others helps you draw closer to Jesus, then seek out these opportunities and participate whenever you can. But it does not make you any less Catholic if you don't participate at all.

> ## The Beloved
>
> *"Why is it so important that you are with God and God alone on the mountain top? It's important because it's the place in which you can listen to the voice of the One who calls you the beloved. To pray is to listen to the One who calls you 'my beloved daughter,' 'my beloved son,' 'my beloved child.' To pray is to let that voice speak to the center of* your being, to your guts, and let that voice resound in your whole being."[38]
>
> HENRI NOUWEN

A great number of devotions dedicated to Jesus, Mary, and various saints have flourished at different times in the Church. For example, in various times and places, people have participated in the Six Sundays of St. Aloysius, the Five Sundays of St. Francis' Stigmata, the Seven Sundays of the Immaculate Conception, the Seven Sundays of St. Joseph, the Ten Sundays of St. Francis Xavier, the Ten Sundays of St. Ignatius of Loyola, and the Nine Fridays in honor of the Sacred Heart. I daresay that probably very few Catholics have firsthand familiarity with all of these, and yet legions of Catholics have participated in each at one time or another.

Devotions are like shoes: the key is fit. You may meet zealots who insist that one particular devotion is the key to a vital spiritual life — and no doubt, it is *for them*. But it may very well *not* be for you. Find things that suit *you*.

7. Accept and Model Unconditional Love

If we want to lead like Jesus, we have to love like Jesus. Perhaps we can never love as much and as perfectly as He loved, but if we wish to model our lives on His, we cannot neglect His call to love. Recall Jesus' response when a young man asked Him which commandment was the greatest:

> He said to him, " 'You shall love the Lord your God with all your heart, and with all your soul, and with all your mind.' This is the greatest and first commandment. And a second is like it: 'You shall love your neighbor as yourself.' On these two commandments hang all the law and the prophets." (Mt 22:37-40)

At the Last Supper, Jesus tells His disciples:

> "I give you a new commandment, that you love one another. Just as I have loved you, you also should love one another. By this everyone will know that you are my disciples, if you have love for one another." (Jn 13:34-35)

Soon after, before going out into the garden of His agony, Jesus ends a heartrending prayer with one last request to His Father: "that the love with which you have loved me may be in them, and I in them" (Jn 17:26).[39]

8. Serve Others

Serving others follows directly from Jesus' command — and His fervent wish and prayer — that we love one another. Love is more than how we feel and how we think. Love is *what we do*. If we love people, we will serve them by looking after their genuine interests, not the least of which is their need to continue growing mentally, emotionally, and spiritually long after their physical growth stops. The commandment to love our neighbor as much as we love our own self calls us to consider his or her legitimate needs just as important as our own. It does us little good to profess faith in Jesus and then not follow His teaching and example. As He said, "Not everyone who says to me, 'Lord, Lord,' will enter the kingdom of heaven, but only the one who does the will of my Father in heaven" (Mt 7:21).

9. Build Community

Some people assume that Christian faith is just a matter of "me and Jesus," and that the Christian life is lived fully when we focus only on trying to assure ourselves that we will spend eternity with Jesus.

Recall Jesus' encounter with a scholar who asked, "And who is my neighbor?" (Lk 10:29). Jesus turns the question on its head by telling him the parable of the Good Samaritan. Jews and Samaritans were traditional enemies. Yet the Samaritan troubled himself to save a Jew. If a Samaritan recognized that he had an obligation to treat a Jew as a neighbor, who then is not our neighbor?

In Matthew 25, Jesus tells us how important the welfare of other people should be to us when He describes His return in glory to judge the world. At that point, He will gather some people in a group and invite them into His Father's kingdom because they have fed Him, slaked His thirst, welcomed Him, clothed Him, cared for Him in illness, and visited Him in prison. Those in the select group are confused. They don't recall doing any of these things for Him. So He

A "Pure Gift"

"This power, the grace of the Spirit, is not something we can merit or achieve, but only receive as pure gift. God's love can only unleash its power when it is allowed to change us from within. We have to let it break through the hard crust of our indifference, our spiritual weariness, our blind conformity to the spirit of this age. Only then can we let it ignite our imagination and shape our deepest desires. That is why prayer is so important: daily prayer, private prayer in the quiet of our hearts and before the Blessed Sacrament, and liturgical prayer in the heart of the Church. Prayer is pure receptivity to God's grace, love in action, communion with the Spirit who dwells within us, leading us, through Jesus, in the Church, to our heavenly Father. In the power of his Spirit, Jesus is always present in our hearts, quietly waiting for us to be still with him, to hear his voice, to abide in his love, and to receive 'power from on high,' enabling us to be salt and light for our world." [40]

POPE BENEDICT XVI

explains, "Truly I tell you, just as you did it to one of the least of these who are members of my family, you did it to me" (Mt 25:40). Clearly, being a faithful disciple of Jesus involves much more than just setting our sights on heaven and looking after ourselves.

Jesus told His disciples:

"Go therefore and make disciples of all nations, baptizing them in the name of the Father and of the Son and of the Holy Spirit, and teaching them to obey everything that I have commanded you. And remember, I am with you always, to the end of the age." (Mt 28:19-20)

This is not a task that a solitary Christian can accomplish alone. Indeed, Jesus' instructions come down to us only because they were recorded and preserved by a community that continued to pass them down through the ages despite the deaths of the apostles and the subsequent deaths of generation after generation of disciples. If we are to respond favorably to Jesus' great commission, we must do it in a community of disciples that will survive until the end of time.

The Church is, in fact, a community of communities, with its most basic constituent element the family, which Pope John Paul II often referred to as the "domestic church." Just as Jesus promises His community of disciples that "I am with you always, to the end of the age" (Mt 28:20), so He tells us that it is in community that we find Him: "For where two or three are gathered in my name, I am there among them" (Mt 18:20). He also says that when someone sins against us, we should turn to the community to help make it right (Mt 18:15-17). Jesus tells us, too, that if we want our prayers of petition granted, we should pray them with others (Mt 18:19). Note, too, that the prayer He taught us begins with "Our Father," not "My Father" (Mt 6:9).

A big part of Jesus' ministry was devoted to building a community of disciples. Had He not done so, what would have happened to His ministry and self-sacrifice? Who would have even known of it after a generation or two? Jesus speaks of Himself as a vine and tells His disciples to think of themselves as the vine's branches: "I am the vine, you are the branches. Those who abide in me and I in them bear much fruit, because apart from me you can do nothing" (Jn 15:5).

A vine and its branches are an interactive, organic whole. Moreover, each branch relies on the vine for life. To think in terms of the health of just one branch — as we do if we think only in terms of our own personal salvation — is to neglect the health of the entire vine, which is Jesus.

The mission of lay Catholics is to *sanctify the world*, not simply to try to somehow earn our individual passage into heaven. In fact, it would literally be a heresy to suggest that we can earn eternal happiness on our own. Clearly, Jesus expects us to live out our Christian calling to *sanctify the world* in community with other Christians. Thus, we have the obligation to look after the welfare of that community and to contribute to its welfare and mission in whatever way we can.

REFLECTION QUESTIONS

- How would I benefit from devoting more time for solitude, prayer, and reading Scripture in my life?
- What little changes could I make in my schedule to have more time for these things?
- How might I benefit more from the opportunities my Church provides me to worship and receive the sacraments?
- What things did I learn in the past to help me develop spiritually that I've since come to neglect? Which ones might help me to lead more like Jesus in the days ahead?

The earth is the LORD's and all that is in it,
the world, and those who live in it.

PSALM 24:1

"Blessed are those servants whom the master finds awake when he comes; truly, I say to you, he will put on his apron and have them sit at table, and he will come and serve them."

LUKE 12:37 (RSV)

Like good stewards of the manifold grace of God, serve one another with whatever gift each of you has received.

1 PETER 4:10

"All is grace."

ST. THÉRÈSE OF LISIEUX

"To be grateful is to recognize the Love of God in everything He has given us."[41]

THOMAS MERTON

Chapter Nine

S²: Called to Be a Steward

At its core, Jesus' call to leadership in our homes, workplaces, churches, and communities is a call to be a servant leader. As Ken Blanchard and Phil Hodges like to say, "Jesus gives us no Plan B." Responding fully to Jesus' call with a servant's heart, head, hands, and habits is a lifelong challenge. In trying to meet that challenge on a day-to-day basis, a practical metaphor may prove helpful: *steward* and the notion of *stewardship*. In this chapter, we consider how serving as a steward helps us more fully respond to Jesus' call for us to be effective Christian leaders.

Basic Reality for Believers

The concepts of *steward* and *stewardship* are basic and primary for anyone who considers himself or herself a believer. No matter what we have — be it power, money, material goods, lofty position, or even life and health — it is not ours to do with simply as we wish. Inherent in the notion of religious belief is the sense that life itself and all good that comes in life are but gifts from God *entrusted to us as servants and stewards* for the common good at least as much as for our own personal good.

If that were not true, why would Jesus tell us that God expects us to "love your neighbor as yourself" (Mt 22:39)? That is a very different directive from "The world is yours — do with it and its creatures as you please." God doesn't give us the earth to do with as we please, either collectively or individually. He gives us *dominion over* the earth and all its creatures (including ourselves) to *look after it all for Him as He would look after it Himself* — which is to say, in love.

Stewardship is a concept that may prove especially helpful for people working in the private sector. Since the turn of the new millennium, we have seen the prosecution of several prominent CEOs after the major public companies they ran imploded in a flood of fraud, causing unspeakably painful losses to all of their stakeholders, including employees, retirees, investors, vendors, and the larger communities in which they did business. Clearly, publicly traded companies are in need of a new model for effective leadership worthy of the massive trust put in their leaders. *Steward* is just such a model.

The word *steward* has both a narrow meaning and a broad one. In the narrow sense, a steward is a person who holds a particular position of service to another person. In the broad sense, a steward is someone who assumes responsibility for things that do not belong to him.

It is the broad notion of steward and stewardship that concerns us here. That sense of steward and stewardship is found in the Genesis account of creation (even though the word itself is not used in the text). There, in the first story of creation, we read:

> Then God said, "Let us make humankind in our image, according to our likeness; and let them have dominion over the fish of the sea, and over the birds of the air, and over the cattle, and over all the wild animals of the earth, and over every creeping thing that creeps upon the earth."

> So God created humankind in his image,
> > in the image of God he created them;
> > male and female he created them.

> God blessed them, and God said to them, "Be fruitful and multiply, and fill the earth and subdue it; and have dominion over the fish of the sea and over the birds of the air and over every living thing that moves upon the earth." God said, "See, I have given you every plant yielding seed that is upon the face of all the earth, and every tree with seed in its fruit; you shall have them for food. And to every beast of the earth, and to every bird of the air, and to everything that creeps on the earth, everything that has the breath of life, I have given every green plant for food." And it was so. God saw everything that he had made, and indeed, it was very good. (Gen 1:26-31)

Stewards in Scripture

The word *steward* does not occur frequently in Scripture. The number of times varies with the translation. In some translations, words like "slave" and "manager" supplant it on occasion. When *steward* does appear, in most instances it's the job description of a peripheral character. One exception is in St. Paul's letter to Titus, where it is used in specific reference to the role of a bishop:

> A bishop, as God's steward, must be blameless; he must not be arrogant or quick-tempered or addicted to wine or violent or greedy for gain; but he must be hospitable, a lover of goodness, prudent, upright, devout, and self-controlled. (Titus 1:7-8)

However, since we are all called to be stewards, St. Paul's advice is relevant to all of us.

The second account of creation (Gen 2:4-25) also makes a brief reference to the role humans are to play in creation when it says: "The LORD God took the man and put him in the garden of Eden to till it and keep it" (Gen 2:15). Whether these stories are understood as historically factual or as metaphorical accounts revealing profound truth about the relationship of humanity to God, it's clear in both accounts that the Creator does not forfeit ownership of creation to humanity. Instead, creation springs from the creative will and breath of God, and as such, it is an *extension* of His own being. Since creation exists only as an extension of God's loving, creative will, so long as creation exists it necessarily *belongs* to Him in the most profound sense of that word. The Creator's ownership of creation is irrevocable.

Genesis tells us that the Creator turns over dominion of the earth to humanity, but clearly this dominion is not absolute. Humanity is not free to do with creation whatever it chooses, as an owner might — either collectively or individually. As Pope Benedict XVI told several hundred thousand young people gathered in Sydney for World Youth Day in July 2008: "Experience shows that turning our back on the

---IN THE CHURCH---

"Whatever You Did to the Least of My People . . ."

After returning from Calcutta in 1986, Pope John Paul II was moved to establish a house of mercy at the Vatican, to be staffed by Mother Teresa's Missionaries of Charity. He was told by bureaucrats that it wasn't possible. They had security concerns about inviting the anonymous poor and vagrants to the Vatican. But the pope persisted, and a building was found within the Vatican that could be used.

The pope blessed its cornerstone on June 17, 1987, and it opened on May 20, 1988. It is known as the Gift of Mary House of Welcome for the Poorest. It includes dormitories for men and women and can serve 70 persons overnight. Two dining rooms and a kitchen feed a hundred homeless people daily.[42]

Creator's plan provokes a disorder which has inevitable repercussions on the rest of the created order." He also sounded a stewardship note when he said, "We have become more and more aware of our need for humility before the delicate complexity of God's world."[43]

If creation were ours to do with as we want, what point would there be in God putting limits on humanity's use of creation as He did with forbidding eating of the "tree of knowledge of good and bad"? It is in this sense of caretaking, not subjugation, that God calls all of us to be *stewards* of His creation. Since He brings all creation into existence as the expression of His infinite love in each moment, it only stands to reason that our role in exercising dominion over creation is supposed to be one of *loving stewardship*. It is in this sense that Christians are called to see themselves as *stewards,* and in this context it is easy to understand how Jesus could summarize the whole of Jewish law in two commandments to love. As stewards, we are accountable to God and to His creation, including especially one another.

St. Paul provides very specific advice regarding what the behavior of a good steward looks like. He says we should hold fast to what Jesus taught, seek goodness and temperance, and strive to be hospitable, just, holy, and self-controlled. At the same time, we should avoid arrogance, irritability, drunkenness, aggressiveness, and greed.

For such behavior to be sustained, a person must become rooted in the realization that the universe does not exist to revolve around his or her wishes, whims, or compulsions, and that the purpose of creation — including especially its people — is not to please and serve him or her. Ultimately, creation is all about God, our Creator and Sustainer, who loves us more than life itself. We are but *stewards*, caretakers, of His marvelous creation. Our role is to *care for it as He would Himself* — which is to say, to look after it in love, putting first and foremost its best interests to sustain life, especially human life. When we do this, we are living out our purpose as loved creatures especially fashioned in the Creator's own image.

People who are self-centered will have great difficulty with this perspective. They do not see themselves as called to serve God or, in the case of nonbelievers, any other mission outside themselves. Instead, they are driven to look after themselves and all their appetites — for status, money, material goods, power, or whatever else they covet. As Ken Blanchard and his co-authors write: "Driven people think they own everything. They own their relationships, they own their possessions, and they own their positions. . . . Called people are very different. They believe everything is on loan — their relationships, possessions, and position."[44] As Christians, we are all called to be stewards. And who can doubt that the world — our families, workplaces, communities, churches, and the planet — would be better off if more of us answered that call?

IN THE COMMUNITY

Guys Gone Wild! Confusing Ownership With Stewardship

The concept of a *steward* is a sensibility badly needed in today's business world. For several years, business news has been rife with reports of men (yes, they have all been males) who were charged with looking after the welfare of public corporations but who behaved like robber barons, brutalizing millions of stakeholders by raiding and robbing the assets of the very corporations they were entrusted to protect and grow.

What is the problem? At the obvious level, it involves greed. These men's lives are models of insatiable appetites gone wild. At another level, these crimes are rooted in pride, for as some of the culprits have admitted, accumulating personal riches and indulging themselves in unspeakable extravagance was how they kept score in the game of success — which they mistook for the purpose of life.

But at a deeper level, their wanton criminal self-indulgence seems to be the natural expression of a flawed understanding of reality. They handled the assets with which they were entrusted *as if the assets were their own.* That is, after all, the prevailing metaphor we use to describe the role of the very top officer in a public corporation. The company is *his.* He has the power to make its final decisions. We regard him — and he comes to regard himself — as the *sole owner* of the corporation.

If that were really the case, CEOs could wallow in self-indulgence until either their assets or their hearts gave out. But because this is not the case, many end up having to hide their skewed view of reality by cooking the books or otherwise lying to investors and other stakeholders. Eventually, reality bites: they have to forfeit their power, fortunes, reputations, and in some instances, even their freedom.

The reality is that the power the top official has in a corporation has been *given* to him by its rightful owners, who hold the company's stock. They are free to take away the power they have given him if they decide it is in their best interests to do so. With that in mind, perhaps we will find a newfound emphasis in business schools on the notions of *steward* and *stewardship* at all levels of the corporate ladder.

REFLECTION QUESTIONS

- Have there been times when I behaved as an owner rather than as a steward in my home, at work, or in the community?

- How did this affect the outcome? Did my actions *Edge God Out* or *Exalt God Only*?
- What things must I change in my life to be a faithful steward of God's creation?
- What little thing can I do immediately to make me more of a steward and less of an owner in one of my roles in life?

When he saw the crowds, he had compassion for them, because they were harassed and helpless, like sheep without a shepherd.

MATTHEW 9:36

"I am the good shepherd. The good shepherd lays down his life for the sheep."

JOHN 10:11

"Turn now to consider how these words of our Lord imply a test for yourselves also. Ask yourselves whether you belong to his flock, whether you know him, whether the light of his truth shines in your minds. I assure you that it is not by faith that you will come to know him, but by love; not by mere conviction, but by action."

POPE ST. GREGORY THE GREAT

Chapter Ten

S³: Called to Be a Shepherd

A second metaphor that sheds light on how Jesus expects us to lead is that of a shepherd. The idea of a leader as shepherd goes all the way back to the Bible's first book, Genesis, when Israel (formerly known as Jacob) refers to God as "my shepherd all my life to this day" (Gen 48:15). Later, Isaiah describes God in a way that recalls the melody of a popular liturgical song: "He will feed his flock like a shepherd; / he will gather the lambs in his arms, / and carry them in his bosom, / and gently lead the mother sheep" (Is 40:11). And perhaps the most famous line in the Book of Psalms reads: "The LORD is my shepherd, I shall not want" (Ps 23:1).

Although the Hebrews thought of God as their shepherd, the title was not reserved only for Him. They recognized that others, acting in accord with God's will, would also serve them as shepherds. Moses reflects this understanding in his concern about finding a successor so "that the congregation of the LORD may not be like sheep without a shepherd" (Num 27:17). Still later, all the tribes of Israel acknowledged that God told David, "It is you who shall be shepherd of my people Israel, you who shall be ruler over Israel" (2 Sam 5:2).

It's also clear that the Messiah for which the Hebrew people waited so long was expected to serve as a shepherd. When Herod hears from the Magi that a new king of the Jews has been born, he assembles all the chief priests and scribes and asks them about the long-anticipated Messiah. They tell him that it has been prophesied that a ruler will be born in Bethlehem " 'who is to shepherd my people Israel' " (Mt 2:6). As Jesus engaged in His public ministry, He came to see Himself as a shepherd. In the Gospel of St. John, He is very direct when He tells His followers:

"I am the good shepherd. The good shepherd lays down his life for the sheep. The hired hand, who is not the shepherd and does not own the sheep, sees the wolf coming and leaves the sheep and runs away — and the wolf snatches them and scatters them. The hired hand runs away because a hired hand does not care for the sheep. I am the good shepherd. I know my own and my own know me, just as the Father knows me and I know the Father. And I lay down my life for the sheep." (Jn 10:11-15)

In this passage, Jesus also makes clear what it means to be a good shepherd and what happens to a flock when it is led by a self-centered shepherd. A good shepherd is willing to lay down his or her own life for the sheep. In other words, a leader worthy of being called a "good shepherd" must be willing to put the welfare of his or her followers ahead of his or her own personal welfare. Notice, too, in this passage that Jesus does not expect such leadership from persons who take on the leader's role only for personal gain. In times of crisis, they will abdicate their leader role and abandon their followers in order to look after themselves. When that happens, there are organizational consequences. As Jesus notes, some of the flock's members scatter — each running off trying to protect itself individually — while the wolves feast.

Another Scripture passage reminds us of the importance of reaching out to care for people individually, one at a time, and hints at the leadership implications of doing so. Jesus tells His disciples:

"If a shepherd has a hundred sheep, and one of them has gone astray, does he not leave the ninety-nine on the mountains and go in search of the one that went astray? And if he finds it, truly I tell you, he rejoices over it more than over the ninety-nine that never went astray." (Mt 18:12-13)

Any good parent understands this passage instantly. In fact, you have *lived* it if you've ever lost track of a child, even for just a few moments, at a parade or in a shopping mall or some other public place. Panic sets in instantly. You can think of nothing else until the child is found. Of course, we can't expect people to care for their co-workers in the same way that they care for their children. But neither can effective organizations be built in a climate of indifference for individuals. People perform better when they believe that they and their contributions are appreciated.

If leaders don't recognize the individual value of each member of the organization, then the members themselves will compensate by becoming fearful or prideful and begin to focus more on their own self-interests. Thus, a good shepherd leader is committed to creating a safe environment where good feedback is encouraged and rewarded, and such a leader recognizes that this is work that one person cannot do alone.[45] That's why effective leaders recognize that leadership must be shared throughout the organization if it is to become all that it might be.

Many Are Called

If Jesus had been history's only good shepherd, there would be little hope for us in this world. Without more good shepherds, all of us would end up as wolves' food. But Jesus' purpose was not just about being a good shepherd Himself. He raised the issue in order to teach others how to be good shepherds. The importance He attaches to this becomes clear when He meets with His disciples for the third time after His resurrection from the dead.

> When they had finished breakfast, Jesus said to Simon Peter, "Simon son of John, do you love me more than these?" He said to him, "Yes, Lord; you know that I love you." Jesus said to him, "Feed my lambs." A second time he said to him, "Simon son of John, do you love me?" He said to him, "Yes, Lord; you know that I love you." Jesus said to him, "Tend my sheep." He said to him the third time, "Simon son of John, do you love me?" Peter felt hurt because he said to him the third time, "Do you love me?" And he said to him, "Lord, you know everything; you know that I love you." Jesus said to him, "Feed my sheep." (Jn 21:15-17)

Some might assume from this account that only Peter, alone among all Jesus' disciples, was called to be a good shepherd.

There's no denying that he has a unique role because Jesus speaks to him individually, one-on-one, rather than addressing all of His disciples at once. But clearly, the other apostles and Jesus' wider group of disciples saw themselves as all called to care for one another as Jesus, the Good Shepherd, had cared for them.

Two Dangers

Some people are reluctant to speak of leaders as "shepherds," even in a metaphorical sense, because they see two real dangers inherent in this perspective. First, thinking of the leader-follower relationship in terms of shepherd and sheep can suggest to leaders and followers alike that followers ought to simply do whatever the shepherd instructs. Anyone who has been around real sheep knows they aren't really docile. When shepherds lead poorly, their sheep are in turmoil. When shepherds lead wisely, their sheep will appear docile — but that is owing to the *relationship* of trust the shepherd has established with his sheep, not to some placid disposition of the sheep.

Jesus Himself addresses what a shepherd must do in order to obtain the apparently docile cooperation of his sheep. In a word, it comes down to *intimacy*.

> He calls his own sheep by name and leads them out. When he has brought out all his own, he goes ahead of them, and the sheep follow him because they know his voice. They will not follow a stranger, but they will run from him because they do not know the voice of strangers. (Jn 10:3-5)

The sheep follow the shepherd not because they are docile by nature, but because he is a good shepherd. The sheep know him and they trust him. If that wasn't the case, they wouldn't follow him. They would run the other way. Apparently, Jesus believes that leadership is something which must be earned.

The second danger is an outshoot of the first. If leaders see themselves as wise shepherds and their followers as dumb animals (or children) who must always be told what to do, it is only a small step for such leaders to assume that the sheep exist to serve the shepherd. This is a real and present danger, confirmed by history. Clearly, it was not Jesus' intent to twist the metaphor in this way. As Jesus uses the image, it is always clear that the long-term welfare of the shepherd is reliant on the well-being of his sheep. If the shepherd makes his own interests paramount — perhaps he's tired and wants to sleep when wolves are prowling, or perhaps he wants to head back to town for a soft bed or to party with friends — his sheep will suffer and so, ultimately, will the shepherd.

In the workplace, self-serving bosses never optimize the performance of their followers, and so the performance of their teams and organizations suffers. Because people are not sheep, stuck in a flock with a single shepherd for life, it's likely that team members with the most skills and aptitude will find other places to contribute, leaving the self-centered leader to be an "employer of last resort" — dependent on the least competent and least committed people who come through the door to stick around and try, generally unsuccessfully, to serve his needs.

Something else happens with leaders who assume their followers are little more than ignorant sheep who have to be directed constantly. They can turn out to be right! Perhaps it is a measure of God's justice, or an indication of His wry sense of humor, but life unfolds in such a way that much of it is self-fulfilling prophecy. If I assume that my next-door neighbor is a jerk and treat him that way, soon enough I will have a lot of empirical evidence that I am right and that he is a jerk. Why? Because the Law of Agriculture prevails: *We reap what we sow.* If we assume that people need constant direction and oversight, soon enough that will become the case. They will lose all initiative — except, perhaps, the initiative to look for another job. Meanwhile, the best that the organization can hope to achieve is minimum compliance.

All metaphors break down at some point, and if people make too much of the notion that people can be thought of as sheep, then the metaphor of leaders as "shepherds" can become downright dangerous. What's critical to remember is Jesus' point in using the metaphor of shepherds and sheep to talk about leadership: *A good shepherd puts the welfare of his sheep ahead of his own welfare.*

There's no denying that sheep are, in fact, relatively dumb and directionless. But that does not give a shepherd an excuse to put his own interests ahead of the interests of his flock. If literal shepherds should not put their wants and needs ahead of the welfare of relatively dumb flocks of animals, how much more essential is it that metaphorical shepherds not put their wants and needs ahead of the welfare of their human flocks?

IN THE FAMILY

A Lesson From the Home Front

The core meaning of Jesus' call for us to lead like shepherds is readily apparent when we consider the leadership role of parents. When a parent's leadership role begins with a baby's birth, the follower is even less capable of looking after itself than is a fully grown sheep. The parent-shepherd must provide everything the baby needs to survive. But as the child grows from a baby into a youth, then into an adolescent, and finally into an adult, its needs change radically — and so the role of the good shepherd/parent must change radically as well.

Initially, we do not encourage a child to walk. Her body isn't ready for that. But then suddenly we are helping her balance while urging and cheering her on. As soon as the child has mastered walking, she needs help staying out of the street. Parents tell the child, "Never ever cross the street." But in a few years parents are taking the child to the curb and teaching her how to cross the road safely because she has to get to school or to a bus or to a friend's house to play. She can no longer continue to grow and blossom if she is restricted to a life within the boundaries of a block.

For many more years, the child is forbidden to drive a car any distance at all, not even in the driveway. Then suddenly her parents are filling out a host of forms, paying some fees, and putting her behind the wheel to learn in a matter of weeks how to navigate crowded expressways. The parents' skeptical insurance carrier demands an extra toll for this, one to be extracted at regular intervals, although not as regularly as tolls for gas, oil, and auto upkeep. Suddenly, parents are investing huge sums so their child can do something that was forbidden only days before.

Eventually, the same children who couldn't walk alone may be sent off into the world or off to college to fend for themselves without any adult supervision.

All of these changes and accompanying sacrifices on the part of parents would seem insane except for one undeniable fact: they are required for a child's development from helpless baby to competent, caring, and contributing adult. Granted, the cycle of parent-child development never goes quite as smoothly as it's described in the barest outline here. And sometimes it does not turn out well at all. On the other hand, it is amazing how well and how often it does work.

Good Discipleship Is More Than Good Intentions

As we said at the beginning of this book, good intentions are important. If we do not start out with the intention to lead like Jesus — if we do not develop a servant's heart — then we will not become a servant leader in the image of Jesus. Yet, as the proverb says, "The road to hell is paved with good intentions." Good intentions alone are not sufficient to lead like Jesus. Christlike leadership requires knowledge, skills, and practice. And since we will all come up short at times, especially when we are learning, we need forgiveness. We need to *give* it, we need to *ask* for it, and we need to *accept* it when it is offered.

For some people, the big problem is forgiving. Others struggle with asking for forgiveness. Still others have great difficulty accepting forgiveness. And still others have trouble with all three aspects of this very important human interaction. Whatever our difficulties, individually and collectively, forgiveness is a requirement of the human condition. So it is worth our efforts to foster more forgiveness everywhere life takes us.

- *Offering forgiveness* is not always easy. Often we are driven to avenge the wrong done to us. Here again Jesus provides us with the ultimate model. Hanging on a cross, His hands and feet burning from the nails that pierced them, gasping for breath as His diaphragm struggled against the relentless force of gravity, contemplating His own death as a criminal, He gazed down upon the men who put him there and begged: "Father, forgive them; for they do not know what they are doing" (Lk 23:34). Forgiving is a difficult thing to do, but we cannot say that we do not have a model for doing it.

• *Asking for forgiveness* can be incredibly difficult, too. If we are driven by pride or fear, we can take refuge in self-righteousness rather than owning up to the harm we have done, however unintentionally. Even if we don't lapse into self-righteousness, it is still hard to admit to ourselves and to others that we are not perfect. For some people, it is well-nigh impossible. If

The Example of Mary

The dangers of framing leader-follower relationships in terms of the parent-child relationship are exactly the same ones that arise when leader-follower relationships are framed in terms of shepherd-sheep relationships. Such a framework can lead to a "paternalistic" approach to leadership: adults are treated like children, which diminishes their freedom, dignity, and ultimately, their development and effectiveness. Shepherds who do not put the needs of their sheep first, parents who do not put the needs of their children first, and leaders who do not put the needs of their followers first will not do their jobs very well and cannot expect optimum outcomes. The relationships will not be especially productive, rewarding, or satisfying for any of the participants. The fact is that in a healthy parent-child relationship, the parent does not persist in treating his or her child *as a child*, but rather *as an individual* whose development needs are constantly changing. That is the true meaning of "paternalistic" leadership — leadership driven by selfless love.

In Scripture, we find what it means to be truly "paternalistic" when God the Father decides He wants to involve a young girl in

His plan for humanity's salvation. He sends an angel to inform a young girl in the little town of Nazareth about His incredible plan to save the world. He could have told the angel to tell Mary to just do what she is told. After all, He is God, all-knowing and all-powerful. God, who doesn't need any reasons, had all the reasons in the world to just compel Mary's compliance. What does He do? He sends a messenger to consult with her.

First, the angel praises her. But instead of simply accepting the compliment, Mary is troubled by the whole encounter. So the angel reassures her. After that, he forthrightly provides her with the details of God's plan, outlining both the short-term and long-term implications for her and for the world. Mary is still wondering. She wants some details. The angel provides them, and again offers some reassurances. Only then does she accede to God's request and reply, "Behold, I am the handmaid of the Lord; let it be to me according to your word" (Lk 1:38; RSV).

Mary's willingness to go along with God's plan has been the focus of much theologizing and meditation over the centuries, but there is another facet to this encounter that provides us with a model for how leaders ought to treat followers. God Himself — all-powerful, all-knowing, all-loving, and focused on achieving the most important task in history — did not demand Mary's obedience. Instead, He chose to share His plan with her, provide her with the reassurances she asked for, and give her the choice of whether or not to cooperate. If God respects a human being that much, how can we justify treating other people as if they are just pieces to be moved around a chessboard at our will? The answer is: As Christians, we can never justify it.

---

asking for forgiveness is something you struggle with, I recommend a thin little book by Ken Blanchard and Margaret McBride called *The One Minute Apology: A Powerful Way to Make Things Better.*[46]

- *Accepting forgiveness* is not always an easy thing either. On the one hand, we can accept it all too easily, without any sense of sorrow or repentance for the pain we have caused. But when we are aware of the harm we have done, and are deeply sorry for having done it, the only thing harder than asking for forgiveness can be accepting it when it is offered — either by God or another person. It's important to accept God's forgiveness as well as the forgiveness that others may offer because when we don't, we are playing God as surely as when we lord it over other people. We are making our own judgment the supreme judgment of the universe. That's not our job, it's not a good place for us to be, and in the end it separates us from the human community, from God, and from the self God gave us to be for our good and His glory.

We all are sinners. We all come up short from time to time. When we acknowledge our sins, when we accept responsibility for the consequences of our action or inaction (whether or not we intended the consequences that occurred), when we resolve to make amends and to go forward mindful of our continued shortcomings, Jesus wishes that we all "go in peace." If forgiving, asking for forgiveness, or accepting it is a struggle in your life, holding you back from a deeper commitment to servant leadership, pray for the grace to keep growing today, and every day that God grants to you, in love.

ON THE JOB

What's Love Got to Do With It?

After speaking in Lexington, Kentucky, to a group consisting mostly of business leaders about the most powerful force in the universe to permanently transform people, a man in the audience raised his hand and offered me some loving advice.

"I really like what you're saying, but if you want to talk about it out in the business world where I am, you're going to have to find another word for it besides *love*."

Everybody laughed. The man had just named the 600-pound gorilla sitting in the middle of the room. Love is all about trusting and selflessness, and we are taught very young not to trust too much. As disappointments and betrayals pile up over the years, we can lose our capacity to trust altogether. In addition, when we speak of love, we imply a commitment, and many people are not all that comfortable making commitments of any kind these days.

Love's problem in today's world was made clear in a humorous way by a series of commercials for Bud Light beer in the mid-2000s. In each vignette, two men are sitting side by side. One has a Bud Light in his hand, and the other is empty-handed. The guy without a beer leans over to the guy with a beer and says, with deep emotion, "I love you, man." Is this a moment of deep, honest intimacy, something that men supposedly find hard to express?

Not exactly. The man with the beer responds instantly, "You're not getting my Bud Light!"

The notions that we should keep our feelings to ourselves and that the only time we should use the word "love" is when we're trying to manipulate someone are all too common in our culture. Part of the problem is that in English we expect the word *love* to cover a lot of things — from our appreciation for a new pair of socks to our willingness to turn our life over to another person in marriage for as long as we live. It's no wonder that we're reluctant to use a word with such broad meaning because it is so open to misunderstanding. Yet, as Christians, we can't avoid it. When asked about the most important expectation God has for humanity, Jesus spoke only of *love* (or its Aramaic equivalent).

The ancient Greeks needed three words to describe our most common definitions of *love,* and perhaps that helped them avoid some of the confusion and discomfort we have with the word. Their words for love were:

- *eros* — passionate love, with sensual desire and longing, although not necessarily sexual in nature; it can be directed at things as well as people that excite our passions; this term is not used in the New Testament.
- *philia* — friendship, kinship, and affinity with communities; it inspires trust and loyalty; a concept developed by Aristotle and used occasionally in the New Testament.
- *agape* — a general affection for people and things that can deepen into a willingness to sacrifice the self; relationships marked by *agape* cause people to hold one

another in high regard, to be appreciative and content, to be self-sacrificial; this is the word used most often in the New Testament that we translate as *love,* including those occasions when Jesus tells us to love our neighbor as ourselves (Mt 22:39) and to "love one another as I have loved you" (Jn 15:12).[47]

Maybe it would be a good idea for us to begin talking about the need for more *agape* in our homes, workplaces, churches, and communities — and perhaps that day will come. But in the interim, it seems that we will have to keep getting by using the term *love,* stopping to briefly explain that we are talking about self-sacrificing love rather than sexual attraction or exploitation.

When it came down to seeking assurances from Peter before Jesus ascended into heaven, the Lord did not ask Peter if he would be conscientious, if he would do a good job of organizing — not even if he would keep Jesus' mission in mind. Instead, Jesus asked just one thing: "Do you *love* me?"

Jesus asks the same question of each of us: "Do *you* love me?" When all is said and done, true Christian discipleship and leadership involves a fundamental decision: *Who or what will I most love?* And ultimately, that decision requires us to make a choice: *Will I be self-centered or God-centered?* It is not a choice we can make once forever. Instead, it is a choice we have to make again and again — in every relationship, in every encounter, and in every other choice that comes to us.

REFLECTION QUESTIONS

- In what roles am I a shepherd entrusted with a flock to protect?
- Given Jesus' description of a "good shepherd," how can I improve my own shepherding roles?
- Which is most difficult for me — offering forgiveness, seeking forgiveness, or accepting forgiveness? What can I do to get better at it?

- Assuming selflessness is the basis for true love, in which roles am I an able lover — and in which relationships do I need to improve my capacity to love?

For as in one body we have many members, and not all the members have the same function, so we, who are many, are one body in Christ, and individually we are members one of another.

ROMANS 12:4-5

"And so amid variety all will bear witness to the wonderful unity in the Body of Christ: this very diversity of graces, of ministries and of works gathers the sons of God into one, for 'all these things are the work of the one and the same Spirit' (1 Cor 12:11)."[48]

SECOND VATICAN COUNCIL

Chapter Eleven

Why S³ Leadership Works

In the past few decades, scholars have begun talking about the organization as an open, living system — as an organism, a *body* — which is a big change from the previously held image of an organization as a piece of machinery. People used to say that we want to hear our organizations "hum" like a well-lubricated machine, or that we want to see them "tick" like a well-made watch. Behind these metaphors is an image we have in our heads of the efficient organization operating as a series of shafts and gears meshing smoothly, so that the machine relentlessly produces whatever it is designed to grind out.

But this image is flawed: it is so simplistic that it blinds us to the reality of organizational behavior. The problem with a mechanical view of organizations is that simple machines can have only one input. If you were to give a watch input from two mainsprings working on the same sets of gears, instead of the watch grinding out the time from second to second, the gears in the watch would be quickly ground up. The same thing happens to people working in organizations where the leaders see organizational behavior in mechanistic terms. The people get ground up.

Unlike a simple machine, the typical organization is handling hundreds, maybe thousands, of inputs simultaneously. In fact, the individual knowledge worker has to constantly deal with several inputs. He or she may have a desk phone, a cell phone, voice mail on both phones, a PDA, a calendar, a desktop computer running several programs and collecting e-mail, a laptop computer doing the same, snail mail, interoffice memos, newspapers, trade magazines, and a doorway or cubicle through which people wander in to offer input in person. Add a few handwritten notes in a shirt pocket and a briefcase full of correspondence and it's clear that most people in organizations are nearly overrun with information input.

Why do organizations spend incredible sums of money to make sure that each of their employees has access to a multitude of inputs? It's not because they want to make sure that their people are constantly frazzled by an overload of incoming data, or that they get to impress their friends who work for other companies. An organization invests in a multitude of inputs so that its members are able to get and share information in order to respond quickly and appropriately to the flow of constant change in the organization's internal and external environments.

Without the information, collaboration, and responsiveness a multitude of inputs makes possible, an organization would soon be unable to produce, respond, or survive. All of the inputs with which the modern organization equips its individual parts — Bill Gates calls this a "neural network" — represent an investment in survival. But because most organizations' leaders operate out of a simplistic paradigm of the organization, instead of *grinding out* production, they *grind up* their parts, which are their people.

Organizations do not work like well-tuned machines. They work like organisms that deal successfully with tens of thousands of simultaneous inputs. It's a brilliant insight. But it's also an ancient one. St. Paul spoke of the Church as a body — the Body of Christ — some 2,000 years ago. The fact that all organizations are bodies — and the Church is the Body of Christ — has two major implications. In order to sustain life, a body requires two things: organic *diversity* and *feedback*.

The Necessity of Organic Diversity

Some of what St. Paul said applies only to the Body of Christ, but some of what he said applies to all organizations. Here, first, is what applies only to the Body of Christ:

> For just as the body is one and has many members, and all the
> members of the body, though many, are one body, so it is with

Christ. For in the one Spirit we were all baptized into one body — Jews or Greeks, slaves or free — and we were all made to drink of one Spirit. (1 Cor 12:12-13)

Elsewhere, Christians learn that we are all brothers and sisters in Christ. But St. Paul's description of us as a single body sharing a

Diversity: God's Way of Doing Things

In the *Catechism of the Catholic Church*, we read that the organic diversity of the Body of Christ is part of God's plan:

> On coming into the world, man is not equipped with every-thing he needs for developing his bodily and spiritual life. He needs others. Differences appear tied to age, physical abili-ties, intellectual or moral aptitudes, the benefits derived from social commerce, and the distribution of wealth (cf. *Gaudium et Spes*, 29.2). The "talents" are not distributed equally (cf. Mt 25:14-30; Lk 19:11-27). These differences belong to God's plan, who wills that each receive what he needs from others, and that those endowed with particu-lar "talents" share the benefits with those who need them. These differences encourage and often oblige persons to practice generosity, kindness, and sharing of goods; they foster the mutual enrichment of cultures. (CCC 1936-37)

The *Catechism* continues by quoting St. Catherine of Siena, who said she heard God say:

> "I distribute the virtues quite diversely; I do not give all of them to each person, but some to one, some to others. . . . I shall give principally charity to one; justice to another; humility to this one, a living faith to that one. . . . And so I have given many gifts and graces, both spiritual and tem-poral, with such diversity that I have not given everything to one single person, so that you may be constrained to prac-tice charity towards one another. . . . I have willed that one should need another and that all should be my ministers in distributing the graces and gifts they have received from me" (*Dial.* I, 7). (CCC 1937)

single life animated by God's own Spirit brings us even closer into a single organic whole. Each of us is a member, with a unique role to play in the life of the body. But that role exists only in relation to the larger Body of Christ of which we are a part. Thus, as the documents of Vatican II tell us: "In the Church there is diversity of ministry but unity of mission."[49]

While it behooves us to consider the unity of mission (purpose) in any organization, St. Paul says that in order to do that we must appreciate the *necessity of diversity* in every body. He states his line of argument in refreshingly down-to-earth language:

> Indeed, the body does not consist of one member but of many. If the foot would say, "Because I am not a hand, I do not belong to the body," that would not make it any less a part of the body. And if the ear would say, "Because I am not an eye, I do not belong to the body," that would not make it any less a part of the body. If the whole body were an eye, where would the hearing be? If the whole body were hearing, where would the sense of smell be? But as it is, God arranged the members in the body, each one of them, as he chose. If all were a single member, where would the body be? As it is, there are many members, yet one body. The eye cannot say to the hand, "I have no need of you," nor again the head to the feet, "I have no need of you." (1 Cor 12:14-21)

The average fourth-grader probably knows more human physiology than anyone knew in St. Paul's day, but when it comes to using the body as a metaphor for the organization, St. Paul is a true master. It is imperative that an organization's "members" work together despite the fact that not all the parts seem to have equal importance. In the body, he notes, there are parts that seem to be "weaker . . . less honorable . . . less respectable . . . and otherwise "inferior" (1 Cor 12:23-24). Yet, in every case, by God's design, compensations are made so "that there may be no dissension within the body, but the members may have the same care for one another" (1 Cor 12:25).

Diversity is necessary in every body because if a body's organs (or "members") were alike, "where would the body be?" A body of all hands or all feet or all eyes or all ears would not be a body at all. Such a thing would not look like a body, and it would not act like a body. Most important, it could not sustain life — which means it could not be a body. In an organic context, diversity is a necessity of unity. As some people might explain today, diversity is *hardwired* into every single body. There are no exceptions.[50]

People in organizations struggle with notions that some departments or positions in the organization are more important than others, and this often undermines "unity of purpose." From Paul's metaphorical perspective, that makes about as much sense as the heart, lungs, and brain getting into a dispute over which is more important to the body's welfare. Obviously, without all the parts working together — each doing what it is designed to do — none of them is any good at all.

We know, of course, that there is something of a hierarchy to the body's parts. We can lose an eye or an ear without losing our faculties of sight or hearing. We can lose more than one finger or toe, even a whole arm or leg, yet still grasp and walk. We can get along without our appendix and our gall bladder, and we can function without one lung or one kidney. The same cannot be said for our brain or our heart. Yet, the critical importance of these two organs is not self-importance. Instead, it is due solely to the services they render to the body. The heart is needed (in conjunction with at least one lung and the circulatory system) to feed the body's cellular composition with oxygenated blood. But the heart has no importance apart from the contribution it makes to the entire body's welfare.

We have not come up with a way to replace one's brain while retaining one's individuality, so perhaps it could be argued that the brain is the body's most important organ. But that would only obscure the roots of the brain's importance. It is utterly dependent on other systems in the body, and by itself can accomplish nothing. The brain is vitally important because it monitors the body's many voluntary and involuntary processes and coordinates them to maintain the body's welfare. In other words, its primary role is *attentive listener*. When a brain cannot monitor or direct the body's systems, it ceases to have any value and the body dies.

If each of the body's organs and systems could contemplate their relative importance, their only rational choice would be *humility*. The importance of each is derived only from the service it renders to the body, and without other parts, none of them is any good at all.

A *servant* leader understands that this is as true of organizations as it is of bodies. So the *servant* leader, especially one who also takes up the other Jesus-like roles of *steward* and *shepherd*, brings a deep sense of humility to the task of leading at home, at work, in the Church, and in the community.

The Organic Necessity of Feedback

A body needs feedback to sustain every one of its life systems. Consider the parable of the radiator and the elbow.

Once, long ago and faraway, a body stood near a hot radiator. As it happened, the body's elbow brushed up against the hot radiator and was burned. The elbow wondered what to do. Should it send a message to the brain and wait for instructions? The elbow feared that it might hear the head say, "Don't bother me. I'll be with you in a bit. I'm doing some complex calculations for my taxes and I can't be distracted right now." The elbow was afraid: "What if the head chews me out for being so stupid?" And in a moment of growing weakness, the elbow also wondered: "What if the other body parts find out and mock me?"

The elbow looked at all its options and decided, "I don't want to get in trouble. I don't want to be yelled at. I don't want to look stupid and be criticized by the head or other body parts." So the radiator continued to burn the elbow until the elbow couldn't stand it any longer and pulled away, badly burned.

It came to pass that an infection set in, and the body became dehydrated as fluids drained through the wound. Meanwhile, since the elbow had kept the whole sorry, painful mess to itself, the body's other parts did not know about the danger. Many of the other parts encountered the radiator individually and were hurt by it. But since all the parts had learned to keep their mistakes and misfortunes to themselves, the body continued to learn about the hot radiator one part at a time until it was burned all over, contracted several infections, and died.

That's a silly story, isn't it? It's ridiculous to think that an elbow might get burned without the rest of the body becoming immediately aware of it. Even something as small as a tiny stone in one's shoe can prompt a foot to send out alarms that preoccupy the whole body.

So what would really happen to a body if its elbow bumped against a hot radiator? In an instant, the elbow would send messages to the arm and shoulders, and together they would pull the elbow from the hot surface and stop further damage. No need to ask the head what to do. Nevertheless, the head would be told instantly about the problem. Messages would shoot throughout the body. The opposite hand would grasp the arm near the burned elbow. In another instant, that hand would turn the arm so that the eye could examine the wound, making it possible for the brain to assess the damage. Meanwhile,

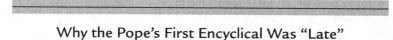

Why the Pope's First Encyclical Was "Late"

Pope Benedict XVI established his scholarly credentials and built a reputation for having a prodigious intellect long before he was elected head of the Catholic Church in 2005. Given his intellect, academic background, and position at the pinnacle of the Church's hierarchy, it was no surprise that he issued an encyclical about a year and a half after being elected to the papacy.

But one thing did surprise some people. The encyclical did not appear when it was expected. While there was no official explanation for the delay, it was widely reported that the encyclical appeared later than expected because the pope took time to get widespread feedback on preliminary drafts before issuing the final version.

Popes are not required by any Church law to get feedback. Nevertheless, Pope Benedict decided it had sufficient value to delay publication of his work.

every body part would have learned to avoid touching the hot radiator and any others like it.

All the parts of an organism behave so quickly and intelligently — each doing what it is uniquely gifted to do — with complete "unity of purpose" because none of the parts is hampered by pride or fear.

A Breakfast of Champions

Ken Blanchard calls feedback "the breakfast of champions."[51] It's easy for us to agree with him when the feedback is positive. Everyone loves positive feedback. But many of us struggle with critical feedback. Effective servant leaders seek out feedback, and when it's critical they try to learn from it. They don't take it all at face value, of course. Just as all positive feedback isn't equally useful or even accurate, so it is with negative feedback. But without accurate, negative feedback, how would we ever improve? Finding and using critical feedback to improve ourselves and our organizations is what separates mediocre performers from champions. If we hope to do better in the future, we need to keep getting feedback that permits us to learn and tells us where and how we can improve.

Organizations generally have a more difficult time getting accurate feedback because pride and fear get in the way. People are proud: they want their bosses and peers to think they are brilliant, not stupid. People are afraid: they don't want to be ridiculed, criticized, punished, or fired. Recognizing this, effective leaders know that one of their major responsibilities is to create environments where people feel safe to give their very best feedback without damage to their reputations, their organizational status, or their relationships with peers and bosses. Bill Gates, founder of Microsoft, has said that the most challenging aspect of his post as the company's leader was making sure that bad news traveled up the system far enough and fast enough that something could be done about it before it did serious harm to the organization. Gates knows the value of feedback, especially negative feedback. So do all good S³ Leaders.

"I Hear You"

Every complex process relies on feedback in ways that we seldom stop to think about. Take the case of the first electronic keyboards. A sales representative came to our office one day and talked about the advantages of his new keyboards to set type in our publishing company's composition room. One of our people asked if the room would be a lot quieter without the constant, loud "click, click, click" that our mechanical keyboards generated. "It'll be quieter, but it won't be silent," he told us. "We tried that, and it was a disaster." He explained that when his company made its first prototypes, there was no sound from the keyboard. Engineers and sales representatives were excited with what they thought was a huge competitive advantage.

But what appealed to engineers and sales representatives was a total disaster for typists. It turned out that while accomplished typists don't rely on visual feedback as much as the rest of us (since they generally don't look at either the keys or at the monitor), they do rely on sound and touch to tell them they have hit keys squarely and with sufficient force to register a keystroke. When the engineers made silent keyboards, they also made useless keyboards. Soon enough, designers were engineering sound back into the devices, because without that feedback, first-rate typists couldn't be productive.

REFLECTION QUESTIONS

- When I see the key organizations of which I am a part as organisms rather than mechanisms, do I see their needs — and their potential — differently?
- What can I do to enhance the organic diversity of the bodies to which I belong?
- Do I nurture environments where honest feedback is encouraged?
- Am I a good listener? How might I improve my listening skills?

Let love be genuine; hate what is evil, hold fast to what is good; love one another with mutual affection; outdo one another in showing honor. Do not lag in zeal, be ardent in spirit, serve the Lord. Rejoice in hope, be patient in suffering, persevere in prayer. Contribute to the needs of the saints; extend hospitality to strangers. Bless those who persecute you; bless and do not curse them. Rejoice with those who rejoice, weep with those who weep. Live in harmony with one another; do not be haughty, but associate with the lowly; do not claim to be wiser than you are. Do not repay anyone evil for evil, but take thought for what is noble in the sight of all. If it is possible, so far as it depends on you, live peaceably with all.

ROMANS 12:9-18

Finally, all of you, have unity of spirit, sympathy, love for one another, a tender heart, and a humble mind.

1 PETER 3:8

"The best test [of a servant leader], and difficult to administer, is: Do those served grow as persons? Do they, while being served, become healthier, wiser, freer, more autonomous, more likely themselves to become servants? And what is the effect on the least privileged in society? Will they benefit or at least not be further deprived?"[52]

ROBERT GREENLEAF

Conclusion

Who can doubt that ours is a world desperately in need of more people committed to lead like Jesus — at home at work, in their communities, and in their churches? If you are committed to a leadership role in any of those places, we hope this book has helped you come to a better understanding of how to proceed.

After facilitating Lead Like Jesus Encounters for over five years, it's clear to me that each of us will find some parts of the journey relatively easy and other parts of it more difficult. For some of us, developing a servant's "heart" seems entirely natural and almost effortless. We have always wanted to serve God and neighbor. But we struggle with one or more of the other dimensions. Our good intentions backfire. We seem to aggravate more people than we attract. We feel the pain of indifference or rejection.

Some of us gravitate to the "head" dimension. We love the conceptual side of life, and we quickly grasp the incredible power inherent in the concepts that are at the core of leading like Jesus. But selflessness may be an alien concept to us. Or our most earnest efforts to apply what we have learned rub hard against the limits of our patience.

Some of us quickly grasp the "hands" dimension as if it were our second nature. We seem to be "natural nurturers," and we look forward to applying what we've learned to help others move closer to their full potential. But we get thrown off task when our efforts are resisted or rejected, or we don't see instant results. Our energy wanes along with our faith in the process and our hope of good outcomes. Soon we lose sight of our own noble intentions.

There also are those of us who warm to discussion of all the "habits" we might adopt. Quite likely, we have already cultivated several good habits, but we focus on how we might foster even more of those discussed. Our focus is so inward that we miss opportunities to exercise Jesus-like leadership in the course of our everyday lives.

Jesus anticipated all of this when He told the parable of the Sower and the Seed. Implicit in His parable are two notions. We are all good seed. But we won't grow into anything of lasting value unless we take root in good soil. For ourselves, that means we need to search for good soil in the choices we make about how to spend our time and with whom we spend it. For others whose paths cross our own, it means we need to strive to serve as good soil, doing all that we can to provide them with safe and nutritious environments where they can grow into all that God intends for them to be.

Life is a journey — a pilgrimage, really. So, too, is our quest to be Jesus-like leaders. As with any journey, there are signposts to guide us along the way. We hope the discussion of a servant's habits is helpful in that regard, and we urge you to revisit that section of this book from time to time, to help keep your focus on how Jesus can help you fulfill your commitment to become an S³ Leader. Resolve to pray and worship often.

Whatever life holds, we invite you to continue your quest to serve the Lord and to lead like Jesus. And we remind you that every trip is easier if you don't attempt it alone. Keep Jesus close to you. And reach out to others. Share with them what you have learned in these pages. Invite them to join you on the journey to lead like Jesus. Together we can achieve what we could never accomplish alone. Finally, here are some suggestions to help you and your traveling companions continue to grow as Jesus-like leaders in your homes, workplaces, parishes, and civil communities.

- **Subscribe to** *The Catholic Leader,* a free e-newsletter that you can arrange to receive at *www.YeshuaLeader.com.* While you're there, explore the Yeshua Catholic International Leadership Institute website to see how you can keep abreast of developments, materials, and learning opportunities designed specifically to help keep you on track in the quest to lead like Jesus.
- **Participate in a Lead Like Jesus Encounter,** where, with other like-minded Christians, you can more deeply explore what it means to lead like Jesus.

- **Visit the Lead Like Jesus website** — *www.leadlikejesus.com* — to keep abreast of new developments, materials, and learning opportunities available to you directly from the Lead Like Jesus movement.
- **Read Ken Blanchard and Phil Hodges' books about leading like Jesus.** Their works include: *Lead Like Jesus: Lessons from the Greatest Leadership Role Model of All Time* (2005); *The Servant Leader: Transforming Your Heart, Head, Hands & Habits* (2003); and *Leadership by the Book: Tools to Transform Your Workplace* (1999, with Bill Hybels). You can order them from *www.YeshuaLeader.com*.
- **Read many other good books about developing effective leadership skills** (by Ken Blanchard and other distinguished authors). Most of the ones we have chosen to feature on our website are very short and focused, so that in just a few hours — sometimes less — you can obtain insights about leadership that will serve you all through life.

———

Finally, brothers and sisters, farewell. Put things in order, listen to my appeal, agree with one another, live in peace; and the God of love and peace will be with you.

2 Corinthians 13:11

Notes

1. *Lead Like Jesus: Lessons from the Greatest Leadership Role Model of All Time*, by Ken Blanchard and Phil Hodges, was first published in 2005. It is currently available in either hardcover or paperback from Thomas Nelson, Inc. All page references are from the Thomas Nelson edition.

2. Pope Benedict XVI, homily on the Solemnity of the Immaculate Conception (Dec. 8, 2005), marking the 40th anniversary of the closure of the Second Vatican Council.

3. Pope Paul VI, apostolic letter *Octogesima Adveniens* (1971), 48.

4. Decree on the Apostolate of Lay People (*Apostolicam Actuositatem*), 3.

5. Dogmatic Constitution on the Church (*Lumen Gentium*), 31.

6. *Octogesima Adveniens*, 48.

7. Decree on the Apostolate of Lay People (*Apostolicam Actuositatem*), 13.

8. Pope John Paul II, address at the Cathedral of St. Mary, San Francisco (Sept. 18, 1987); emphasis in original.

9. Tertullian, *Apology*, Chapter 39.

10. *Lead Like Jesus*, p. 23.

11. Mary Rita Schilke Korzan, "When You Thought I Wasn't Looking," copyright © 1980, used with permission of the author. For information about the author and her work, visit her website: *www.onceuponapoem.com*.

12. Cited by Robert Kreitner and Angelo Kinicki in *Organizational Behavior*, 7th ed. (New York: McGraw-Hill/Irwin, 2007), pp. 282-285.

13. Quoted in Bennett J. Sims, *Servanthood: Leadership for the Third Millennium* (Lanham, MD: Cowley Publications, 1997).

14. George Weigel, *Witness to Hope: The Biography of Pope John Paul II* (New York: HarperCollins, 1999), p. 260.

15. Pope John Paul II, Letter to Priests (Holy Thursday, 1990).

16. Jim Collins, *Good to Great: Why Some Companies Make the Leap . . . and Others Don't* (New York: HarperBusiness, 2001), p. 20. Collins has also published a 42-page booklet, *Good to Great and the Social Sectors: Why Business Thinking Is Not the Answer* (New York: HarperCollins, 2005), that applies his research to not-for-profit organizations.

17. Ibid., p. 20.

18. *Witness to Hope*, p. 95.

19. Robert K. Greenleaf, *Servant Leadership: A Journey Into the Nature of Legitimate Power and Greatness*, 25th anniversary ed. (Mahwah, NJ: Paulist Press, 2002).

20. Pope John Paul II, remarks to bishops of Pennsylvania and New Jersey, *ad limina* visit (Sept. 11, 2004).

21. Pope Benedict XVI, *Jesus of Nazareth* (New York: Doubleday, 2007), pp. 33-34.

22. See "Part One: Paradigms and Principles" in Steven R. Covey, *The 7 Habits of Highly Effective People* (New York: Simon & Schuster, 1989), pp. 3-24.

23. See also Matthew 10:39 and 16:25, Mark 8:35, Luke 9:24, and John 12:25.

24. Gregory F. Augustine Pierce, *The Mass is Never Ended: Rediscovering Our Mission to Transform the World* (Notre Dame, IN: Ave Maria Press, 2007), p. 18.

25. Statement by Warren Bennis (a pioneer in the field of leadership studies), as quoted by Morgan McCall and George Hollenbeck.

26. Scott Blanchard and Drea Zigarmi conducted a major study that distinguished between "strategic leadership" (vision) and "operational leadership" (application). After reviewing hundreds of studies from 1980 to 2005 and their own research data, they concluded: "The real key to organizational vitality is operational leadership." For a more complete discussion of these findings, see Ken Blanchard & Associates, *Leading at a Higher Level: Blanchard on Leadership and Creating High Performing Organizations* (Upper Saddle River, NJ: Prentice Hall, 2007), pp. 255-258.

27. *Witness to Hope*, p. 262.

28. Ibid., pp. 262-263.

29. These changes were reported in a dispatch by Cindy Wooden for Catholic News Service on March 1, 2006.

30. Allen Randolph and Ken Blanchard, "Empowerment is the Key," in *Leading at a Higher Level*, p. 67.

31. Peter F. Drucker, *Managing the Non-Profit Organization: Principles and Practices* (New York: HarperCollins, 1990), pp. 18-19.

32. They call this "The Way of the Carpenter" in their book *Lead Like Jesus*, which I highly recommend.

33. Ken Blanchard and Phil Hodges discuss this important aspect of servant leadership in *Lead Like Jesus*, pp. 138-139; Ken and several co-authors discuss it more comprehensively in *Leading at a Higher Level*, chapter 7, "Partnering for Performance," pp. 117-143.

34. *Lead Like Jesus*, p. 154.

35. Dogmatic Constitution on the Church (*Lumen Gentium*), 11.

36. Dogmatic Constitution on Divine Revelation (*Dei Verbum*), 11.

37. Ibid., 12.

38. Henri Nouwen, "Moving from Solitude to Community to Ministry," *Leadership* (Spring 1995); emphasis added.

39. As an example of a Church leader providing us with helpful commentary, Pope Benedict XVI devoted his first encyclical, *Deus Caritas Est* ("God Is Love"), to the topic of what it means to love. Since the English word "love" is commonly used to encompass the meanings of several distinct words and

concepts in Greek, this encyclical can serve as a very practical guide in helping people understand more deeply what Jesus was telling the young man.

40. Pope Benedict XVI, World Youth Day homily (July 20, 2008), Randwick Racecourse, Sydney, Australia.

41. Thomas Merton, *Thoughts in Solitude* (New York: Farrar, Straus, and Giroux, 1958), p. 33.

42. *Witness to Hope*, p. 566.

43. Pope Benedict XVI, welcoming address at World Youth Day (July 17, 2008), Sidney, Australia. For the complete text, see Australian Catholic Bishops Conference, *www.acbc.catholic.org.au.*

44. *Leading at a Higher Level*, pp. 259-260.

45. There is, perhaps, no better illustration of the importance of this aspect of leadership than the thin but remarkable book *Leadership Is an Art* (New York: Doubleday, 1989), written by Max DePree while he was CEO of the incredibly profitable furniture company Herman Miller, Inc. Said DePree: "The first responsibility of a leader is to define reality. The last is to say thank you. In between the two, the leader must become a servant and a debtor" (p. 11). DePree provides a superb example of how a leader can obtain optimum organizational performance by respecting the dignity, freedom, gifts, and creativity of everyone in the organization.

46. *The One Minute Apology: A Powerful Way to Make Things Better* (2003) by Blanchard and McBride can equip you with a new, incredibly powerful leadership tool and change your life dramatically in about an hour. If you haven't read it yet, I heartily recommend that you do.

47. For an excellent discussion of the various kinds of love and how each has a place in human experience, see Pope Benedict XVI's first encyclical, *Deus Caritas Est* ("God Is Love").

48. Dogmatic Constitution on the Church (*Lumen Gentium*), 32.

49. Decree on the Apostolate of Lay People (*Apostolicam Actuositatem*), 2.

50. As a matter of biological precision, single-cell organisms might seem to be an exception. But if so, they are not a particularly relevant exception in the higher order of things such as human life and leadership.

51. Kenneth Blanchard, Ph.D., and Spencer Johnson, M.D., *The One Minute Manager* (New York: William Morrow, 1982), p. 99.

52. Robert Greenleaf, *The Servant as Leader* (Westfield, IN: Robert K. Greenleaf Center [now Greenleaf Center for Servant Leadership], 1970, June 1982).

Acknowledgments

First, I have to acknowledge the contributions of my wife, Jane, who in addition to looking after me in good times and bad, in sickness and in health, has put up with me for over 42 years and served as my wise and faithful critic, supportive sage, and proofreader throughout. She even refined the graphics for this book.

I'm also grateful to all my children, their spouses, and fiancés — all bright, caring, and helpful people — for their love, encouragement, and helpful feedback. Special thanks to my son Erik, who negotiated the contract for this book; his wife, Robin, who designed the logo for the Yeshua Catholic International Leadership Institute, and my son Owen Jason, who designed and maintains the Yeshua Institute's website. I'm also thankful for my extended family members — more than 100 strong — and most especially my mother, Joan, for encouraging me, loving me unconditionally, and for making sure I never take myself too seriously.

I'm grateful to Phil Hodges and Ken Blanchard, co-founders of the Lead Like Jesus movement, for all the work they have done and for so graciously consenting to let us incorporate that work in this book. I owe a huge debt to their entire Lead Like Jesus team, beginning with Phyllis Hendry and Karen McGuire, but certainly not ending with them, for all their support and encouragement.

I'm honored to acknowledge the important contributions of Richard Kunnert, a fellow at the Yeshua Catholic International Leadership Institute and my closest colleague in the Lead Like Jesus movement. Dick insisted from the very beginning that any Catholic presentation of Lead Like Jesus must include prominent mention of the laity's role to sanctify the world — and then he did much of the research to make that section of this book possible.

I'm grateful to the many lay people whose insights and feedback have contributed to the development of this book, and most especially my ministry colleagues Michael Cieslak and Wayne Lenell, both fellows with the Yeshua Institute; Deacon Patrick Moynihan; and best-selling Catholic authors Matthew Kelly and Patrick Lencioni.

This is an opportunity to thank all my teachers, but most especially Sister Ann Walters, C.S.A., Ray Stroik, Larry Fedewa, and special mentor Frank Wood. I should also include among my teachers all the people with whom I've worked over the years. Their energy, devotion to mission, and courageous feedback have been essential in helping me get to where I should go and redirecting me when I have veered off course. I am also grateful to distinguished publishing pros Gregory Pierce and Joe Durepos, who encouraged me to expand my original plans for this book and offered me invaluable guidance and encouragement. Thanks, too, to dear friend and diligent proofreader Dan McCullough.

I'm indebted to the many priests who have inspired me with their selfless ministry, especially Monsignors Eric Barr, Thomas Brady, Robert Hoffman, and William Schwartz, as well as Fathers David Beauvais, Eugene Hemrick, Mike Librandi, Alfred McBride, O.Praem., William Schuessler, and most especially, my friend Matt (Jerry) Walsh, O.P., a loving missionary, evangelist, and priest for more than 50 years.

I'm also grateful to the many bishops who have befriended and encouraged me over the years, most especially Bishop Arthur J. O'Neill, who introduced me to ministry; Bishop Thomas G. Doran, my own bishop and colleague in ministry for more than a quarter of a century; Bishop Joseph A. Galante, who first invited me to active ministry on a national scale; Bishop Gerald F. Kicanas, who offered me encouragement and guidance from the start; and Bishop Francis J. Kane, episcopal adviser to the Yeshua Catholic International Leadership Institute.

Words cannot fully express my gratitude to the team at Our Sunday Visitor Publishing Division, including especially president and publisher Greg Erlandson, editorial director Beth McNamara, acquisitions editors David Dziena and Bert Ghezzi, Ph.D., manuscript editor Woodeene Koenig-Bricker, book project editor George Foster, cover designer Lindsey Luken, and interior designer Sherri Hoffman, for their vision, faith, support, and guidance in this enterprise.

Of course, I'm grateful to you, dear reader, for your time and interest — and for whatever you ultimately do to lead like Jesus as a

143